JOYCE'S WAY

JOYCE'S WAY

Finding Normality Despite Disability

Susan Klein, M.Ed.

PHOTO CREDITS:
(ii) family photo, Rob Berkley
p. 13 wedding, Norman Partington
p.127, Alan and Joyce, Stan Hill

COVER ILLUSTRATION AND ILLUSTRATION IN PHOTO ON P.(VI)BY JOHN LAMB
COVER DESIGN BY HAL BRIGISH
BOOK DESIGN BY JENNIFER DADDIO / BOOKMARK DESIGN & MEDIA INC.
PRINTED AT SHERMAN PRINTING

PUBLISHER'S CATALOGING-IN-PUBLICATION DATA

Names: Klein, Susan, 1951- | Brigish, Alan, 1942- photographer.
Title: Joyce's way : finding normality despite disability / Susan Klein, M.Ed. ;
[photographs by Alan Brigish].
Description: 1st edition. | West Tisbury, Massachusetts :
brigishEYEproductions, [2018] | Includes bibliographical references.
Identifiers: ISBN 9780692138434
Subjects: LCSH: Brigish, Joyce--Family. | Parents of children with disabilities. |
Down syndrome--Patients--Family relationships. | Down syndrome--Patients--Care.
Classification: LCC HQ759.913 .K54 2018 | DDC 649.151--dc23

Dedicated to my amazing children,

Cy, Hal, and Jackie,

who managed to survive the crazy years of our early lives,

thanks mainly to their wonderful mother,

and my best friend,

Joyce

—AB

To all who have been embraced by inclusion

and felt their hearts soar

—SK

JABBERWOCKY

BY LEWIS CARROLL

'Twas brillig, and the slithy toves
    Did gyre and gimble in the wabe:
All mimsy were the borogoves,
    And the mome raths outgrabe.

"Beware the Jabberwock, my son!
    The jaws that bite, the claws that catch!
Beware the Jubjub bird, and shun
    The frumious Bandersnatch!"

He took his vorpal sword in hand;
    Long time the manxome foe he sought—
So rested he by the Tumtum tree
    And stood awhile in thought.

And, as in uffish thought he stood,
    The Jabberwock, with eyes of flame,
Came whiffling through the tulgey wood,
    And burbled as it came!

One, two! One, two! And through and through
    The vorpal blade went snicker-snack!
He left it dead, and with its head
    He went galumphing back.

"And hast thou slain the Jabberwock?
    Come to my arms, my beamish boy!
O frabjous day! Callooh! Callay!"
    He chortled in his joy.

'Twas brillig, and the slithy toves
    Did gyre and gimble in the wabe:
All mimsy were the borogoves,
    And the mome raths outgrabe.

Preface/Acknowledgements

In the late spring of 2016, Joyce Brigish called with the news of a devastating diagnosis and asked if I would write the story of raising her and Alan's first child, Cy, who had been born with Down syndrome—the central story of her life. Joyce was in the middle of her chemotherapy rounds when we set our interview schedule, not knowing how long she had to live. By the end of June 2016, we had completed seven interviews featuring Joyce and family and friends. Though all agreed she was passionately undeterred from her mission to change the world through her advocacy for people with disabilities, each person I spoke with revealed other aspects of Joyce. She was a formidable opponent to those who would hold tight to the status quo of marginalization, yet she admitted that she was somewhat shy. Her training as a math teacher and love of the subject might suggest she was a linear thinker, yet she was a sculptor and had an eye for design. She had boundless energy and stamina, it seemed, though she battled her own medical problems for many years; her stoic nature and dedication to healthy eating and exercise revitalized her in her daily fight to improve life for all. She was warm and caring and gracious, but when it came to helping people with disabilities learn the parameters of behavior and good manners to help level the social playing field, she was unmovable. She was a diligent volunteer and forward-thinking leader in a variety of organizations over the years, yet, with Joyce, it was always family first. Though I'd known Joyce since 2008, so much of who she was I learned from those who deeply love her.

Without the saved reports, correspondence, and the scrapbooks filled with articles that Joyce compiled over the years, her story could not have been told in this way. The narrative is enhanced by Alan's seemingly boundless cache of family photos. One senses the deeper layers of who Alan is by how he frames his subjects in his camera lens, capturing them in their true light.

A book only comes into being with the help of many. My gratitude is extended to former Camp Jabberwocky director and current board member John Lamb for the cover art; to Hal Brigish for the cover design; to

Jennifer Daddio for the book design; to transcriptionist Sara Crafts, for her flexibility; and to Susanna Sturgis, who, with kind words and good humor and, seemingly, the entire Chicago Manual of Style compartmentalized in her head, edited this manuscript.

Hal's and Jackie's time and attention to the details of growing up were invaluable, as were the conversations and contributions from dear Brigish family friends, Susan Grunthal, Judy Machanik, Phyllis Bertin, Dr. Mark Bertin, Cathy Morton, Eileen Shaw, Sam Simcoe, Adriana Stadecker, and Olive Tomlinson.

Thanks to storyteller Elizabeth Ellis, author Clark Hanjian, special education teacher Alison Pearce, and optometrist Dr. George A. Santos Jr. for their time and attention to my requests.

And special thanks to Alan for commenting, clarifying, and reading every word of this manuscript several times, for his lovely photographs, good friendship, and his patience (in all our projects) with my creative process.

To Cy for his courage and kindness, his wonderful sense of humor, and my indelible nickname. And of course, to Cy and Joyce together for creating a unique relationship, bold and adoring and steadfast, always the stuff of good story. Their shared life transcended the delectable but mundane realities of the five senses and trail-blazed the sometimes illuminating, sometimes perilous pathways of the realm of the non-ordinary where one's heightened awareness of another guides action. With the help of a host of friends, family, and communities, the lane where mother and son gained the footing to be ambassadors for change became a Moebius-strip thoroughfare, where they made headway on issues only to meet themselves coming round the curve on those issues once again in a continuous loop of learning and teaching, striving and achieving—and against overwhelming odds, benefitting the lives of so many.

Susan Klein
Oak Bluffs, MA
June 6, 2018

Chapter 1

2015

On a sweltering evening in 2015 with 95 percent humidity and no rain, the Studio at Camp Jabberwocky was crammed with an enthusiastic audience who had just enjoyed the annual August Show put on by an even more enthusiastic ensemble of actors from the camp. As the applause died down, and the overheated playgoers slipped out into the sticky air, I headed for Cy Brigish, a camper with nearly four decades of camp experience. This was the highlight of his year—every year.

Cy was standing talking to his parents, Joyce and Alan, as they sat in two metal chairs, congratulating him on the success of the play. Cy was dressed in a costume he'd chosen himself: striped pants, a white tuxedo shirt, bow tie, and powder blue tuxedo jacket. Though this was a lot of layers for the stage lights and the humid August night, Cy hadn't broken a sweat.

"The show was just wonderful, Cy," I said, "and the costumes—yours in particular—were such a feast for the eyes."

"I love this jacket!" he said. "But you know what the best part is?"

"What?"

Spreading his arms wide to include Alan and Joyce in his embrace, Cy said, "I have my parents with me tonight."

Chapter 2

1968

Cy arrived fifty years ago, a child with Down syndrome, many additional disabilities, and a future of medical procedures and complications that would bring the most stoic beings to their knees. But his natural gifts, his consistent social training, his mother's adamant persistence in the advocacy of the inclusion of people with disabilities in family life, recreation, education, and community along with a grand dose of shared love have created a man with whom it is a delight to associate. What possibilities Joyce may have imagined, what roadblocks and challenges she knew her family would have to meet and overcome, did not deter her from making the world and her son's world a better place. The by-product has been awareness-raising and life-changing experiences for people with disabilities as well as those who participated as volunteers or witnesses, and even those who were perpetrators of ignorance or ill will—possibly some whose own shortcomings were not so apparent.

Joyce was resistant to the proclamation of Cy's limited capabilities, consistent in his social and intellectual training, and relentless in her advocacy for everyone with special needs to be included, to be seen, to be affirmed, to be loved. Joyce's family—her husband Alan, Cy himself, and his younger siblings, Hal and Jackie—have been a continuous support in those efforts as she fought long and hard for the rights of people who are different, the right to be included without being pre-judged or dismissed outright. That support and love and the clear evidence of the benefits reaped by the Brigishes operating as a family unit all add up to a model of how we can change the world. Our guide is Joyce Brigish, a remarkable woman.

Chapter 3

ENGLAND

Joyce's Pregnancy—1967

Joyce (née Hirshovitz) and Alan Brigish had moved to England in 1965. Two years later they were pregnant with their first child. Alan's parents, Harry and Fanny, and Joyce's mother, Dora, still lived in South Africa. Joyce's father, Matthew, had died just before the wedding. So they had little parental support in proximity, but a good friend of Alan's parents, Freda Goldblatt, lived nearby.

In the area where the Brigishes lived, each community had a baby clinic and Joyce went to the one nearby to hear about "the latest and the best of everything" and to meet other women who would be giving birth around the same time in the spring.

During Joyce's pregnancy, the doctors at first predicted that she would have a big baby, and that she would have a very easy delivery. Though she spent a great deal of time in the small cottage hospital, the doctors continued to assure her she would deliver easily. But the pregnancy was very difficult and Joyce suspected her body might have been trying to abort.

An Uncanny Prenatal Conversation

During her pregnancy, Joyce said to her pediatrician, "You know, I may be carrying a Downs child, or a child with a disability."

He said, "Why in heaven's name are you saying that?"

While Joyce was at college studying to become a teacher, she had taken a psychology course and focused on people with Down syndrome, which she'd found interesting. So she knew the statistics, and in her group of mothers-to-be, everyone else had already had at least one healthy child. Though a variety of disabilities can be present at birth, she just happened to choose Down syndrome in that conversation with her doctor.

She told him, "You know, I'm prepared for it, because I know a lot about Downs kids." Recounting the story years later, she recalled, "He was appalled and my family was appalled that I could say such a thing. But Alan didn't begrudge me my thoughts; he just said, 'Well, we'll wait and see.'"

Cy is Born — 1968

Just before noon on the 17th of April, Joyce, whose water had not broken, was induced, which did take a predictable course. Forty hours of labor later, the doctor had to concede that his prediction had been wrong: an easy birth this was not. Labor was grueling, and Joyce said, "They didn't try and do anything to help the situation."

But into the world had come "a very well-formed pretty baby—full-faced with sort of a semi-smile on his face," and they named him Cyril—Cy for short.

As soon as he could, Alan sent a telegram to South Africa:

GRANDMA GRANDPA
BORN 3.25 AM 19TH WEIGHT UNCERTAIN
MUMMY MARVELOUS DADDY DELIGHTED
LOVE CYRIL QUINTIN

He immediately followed up the telegram with an aerogramme describing the beautiful baby, and adding: "Joyce reckons that the actual birth itself was peanuts in comparison with that last 8 hours."

In Joyce's first letter to her parents on April 22, she describes a four-day-old Cy in glowing terms—"a chubby-cheeked, gorgeous baby"—and credits Alan with getting her through the forty-hour ordeal. In those days, fathers were not allowed to hold the baby for ten days.

Early Days in the Hospital

A most appealing cherub he was, but this eight-pound baby boy couldn't nurse. "They said I had to make like a cow, but *this* cow didn't work." The baby simply couldn't suck, and had to be fed with a dropper as he didn't do well with a bottle nipple either. This had upset Joyce deeply. Eventually, after some initial distress in feeding, Cy would drink for about ten minutes.

After a number of days, Joyce was moved to a private room, which was

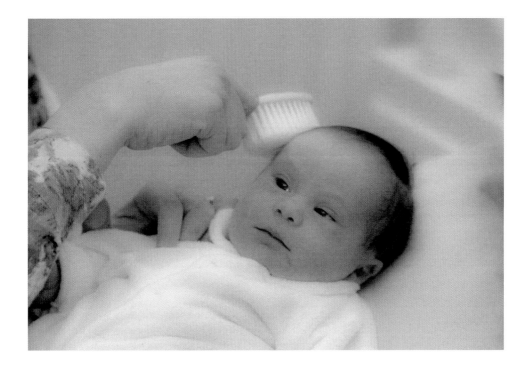

an unusual event in the National Health Service. Joyce could hear the nurses whispering, but couldn't make out what they were saying. She did know she was being treated differently than the other mothers, which brought her to tears.

Alan went to see the matron to ask why Joyce had been isolated. The nurse skirted the issue until Alan finally said, though he had no idea where it came from, "Well, is he Mongoloid"[1] (which was the term used for Down syndrome at the time). The nurse answered in the affirmative but would say no more except that Alan would need to speak to the doctor, and that might take a while. So he sat down to wait.

Discovering Cy's Condition

When two doctors had confirmed that Cy had Down syndrome, one said, "Therefore, there is little sense in raising any false hopes." They recommended that Joyce and Alan undergo testing to establish whether one or both of them carried the genetic anomaly associated with Down syndrome. The results would include a recommendation—or not—"for expanding their family naturally."

After the meeting with the doctor, Alan decided to keep the news from

---

1 The term "mongolism" is removed from most, but not all, references. Mongolism references in scientific literature persisted into the 1970s. Howard-Jones, N. On the diagnostic term "Down's disease". *Med. Hist.* 23, 102–104 (1979). https://www.ncbi.nlm.nih.gov/pmc/articles/PMC1082401/pdf/medhist00100-0117.pdf

Joyce until they took the baby home several days later. That situation was hard on them both. Joyce recalled her response: "Oh, my God! I was devastated. I understood it because I was a teacher and I'd specialized in Down syndrome in my psychology class. So I understood it, and I was angry that they'd left it so late to tell us. I understood—I immediately looked at his hands and his feet and his ears, and his tongue.

"Down syndrome children have a cross-hatch of lines on the palms of their hands and the bottom of their feet. Their tongues are large and their ears have extra crevices. Baby Cy had all those attributes—and he couldn't suck, which is typical. Feeding him liquids was very difficult, and when solid food was introduced, he had to learn to eat."

Friends and Family React and Advise

The thinking—and the general practice of the day—was to institutionalize children with disabilities such as Cy's. Joyce was adamant when she said that such practices were about the welfare not of the children, but rather of the parents. About Cy, she said, "They just felt that this child was going to be in the way of the community, basically. So let's keep him at bay." The family doctor recommended a meeting at the Hospital for Sick Children on Great Ormond Street.

Letters of concern and advice flew back and forth between Alan's and Joyce's parents and friends of the family, all concerned with Alan and Joyce's future, hoping they could influence the couple's decision as to where Cy would live out his life. One friend of the Brigish family and great support to Alan and Joyce was Freda (Fred), who also lived in London. She wrote rambling letters of love and concern to the Brigishes in Johannesburg encouraging a united front to convince Alan and Joyce to give Cy up, and as soon as possible. She knew Alan well enough to know that whatever the couple's decision, Alan would thoroughly research every option "to within a fare-thee-well."

Fred held strong opinions and made dire predictions to Alan's parents in a letter on May 15, thoughts she had already shared with Alan in her no-nonsense way.

> "It would be most unfair to [the] family if they had a retarded first child . . . because the younger children would have a tough time and Joyce would have one hell of a time looking after the retarded child, and wouldn't be able to devote the time or energy to the normal children, and god knows normal children are difficult enough to bring up properly. When the other older children were young they too would be backward because they would imitate the older child and it would be gruesome. To them that would be the norm. When they grew a little older then they would resent the older child because then they would have discovered that he wasn't normal and they would be ashamed of him, and when they brought their friends to the house, then the friends would be cruel and this would be like a knife into Joyce, however strong she is. That is the future family."

To give Fred her due, she explained in the letter that she was not cold or inhuman, but that it was difficult to include the emotions and nuances of the conversation.

Decision

Thinking at the time about a Down syndrome child was much different than it is today. Institutionalizing the child was standard, and as Alan said, "There was no thought given to the child's future of any kind at any level." Joyce followed with "So in general, most people didn't want to acknowledge him, and just basically said to us, 'Why keep him here when you can do so many better things without him?' And I experienced that with the medical profession as well. The worst part was the family rejecting him. I had two friends in the community who are still close friends today, and they didn't feel the way that everybody else felt."

Acquaintances of a cousin of Alan's in London called up to introduce themselves in mid-1968. They were the parents of a little girl with Down syndrome. They'd heard that Cy had been born and they brought their daughter

along to meet Alan and Joyce—so that they could realize "it's worth keeping this child." The two families got on well and would become very close friends for many years, with the children attending each other's birthday parties.

Alan was adamant that Cy would not be institutionalized; they would not "take the easy way out." Fred wrote to Alan's family, "To give away one's child is *not* the easy way out, it will be the most difficult thing . . . to do in life, and they will have to live with it for the rest of their lives."

Alan hit the roof, claiming he didn't want anyone's sympathy. Fred tried to explain that it was not sympathy but rather compassion that people felt for them. Needless to say, beyond the situation, the discussions themselves were stressful as medical and family's and friends' opinions abounded, trying to persuade them.

Fred predicted the end of Joyce and Alan's relationship because of the child—repeatedly stressing that the strain would be too much, especially for Joyce. Alan disagreed. Time would prove Alan correct. Fred, for all her loving concern for them, had sorely underestimated the couple—their shared love and moral compass, Alan's dedication to providing for his family, Joyce's complete disdain for being told what she should or should not do when she knew better, their history of acting on their beliefs—and what no one knew yet: that Cy had come into the world with no small degree of charm and personality.

Chapter 4

THE 1960s: JOYCE AND ALAN'S ACTIVISM IN SOUTH AFRICA

On the topic of genetics, let's just say that bucking the status quo was in both Joyce's and Alan's DNA.

Neither Joyce's nor Alan's family believed in the hideous system of apartheid, and, in fact, both defied it. Joyce's father was a miller, her mother a nurse. Her father hired a black accountant, because he felt "there was no reason not to," though it most assuredly was not acceptable in the apartheid system. Alan's father, Harry, a lawyer, hired a young black lawyer to work for him, one Nelson Mandela.

In his political career, Harry was a founding signatory of the charter for the new political party, the Progressive Party, which today is known as the Democratic Alliance and is the official opposition to the African National Congress (ANC).

Harry stood for parliament in a heavily Afrikaans neighborhood, as a symbol. He lost, of course. A few years later, he stood for provincial council (the regional parliament), and lost by four hundred votes.

While still in South Africa, Alan and Joyce—both passionately opposed to apartheid—did what little they could to fight the system, hanging posters and attending regular political action meetings of the Progressive Party— South Africa's liberals who were the left wing of the all-white parliament. Their only legitimately elected member of parliament for thirteen years was Helen Suzman, and Alan was the chairman of her constituency's youth committee.

Joyce recalled, "There was a big movement against apartheid among a certain group of people. We used to raise money for anti-apartheid projects. We'd have a social with both black and white people, but we'd always have to have somebody at the door, vigilant of any police that would be lurking around."

Alan added, "We'd put up posters and the opposition would tear them down, and put up theirs. Then we'd go back and tear theirs down and put ours back up. The police once caught us in the act and threatened us."

Alan was ambitious and forward-thinking, single-minded, strong-willed, and tough. Both he and Joyce were intelligent, though their creative bents were in different directions, Alan's in melding science and business, Joyce's in art and teaching. They also had mathematics in common. Joyce was tender, passionate, supportive, and patient.

Alan's ambition was "to be involved in the evolution of computers," for which he saw no future for himself in his home country; he felt compelled to emigrate. He spoke to Joyce, who felt the same. So, he told Joyce he was going to graduate and leave. She said she wanted to leave as well. Alan said England, she said the same. So he proposed to her in 1964, and suggested they "move to England and get married" to avoid the logistics of a big wedding. As planned, Alan went to England and landed a job. At the end of the following academic year, Joyce graduated. The wedding date was set. Joyce and her mom, Dora, with wedding dress "in hand," boarded a Union Castle steamship out of Cape Town and headed for Britain. Joyce's father, Matthew, and Alan's parents, Harry and Fanny, were scheduled to fly later. While Joyce and Dora were on the ship, Matthew tragically died in his sleep. Through many intercontinental phone calls, the information at last reached the captain of the ship, who informed Dora and Joyce when they docked at Las Palmas in the Canary Islands. The women flew back to Johannesburg,

which they could only do by way of London. During their five-hour layover, they were met by Alan and Joyce's brother Ivan, who lived in London. Then the two women took a red-eye to Johannesburg. There they held a service for Matthew. Harry and Fanny, Dora and Joyce made arrangements for the wedding. Alan flew in later in the week and he and Joyce were married. Peter Grunthal, Alan's oldest friend, was a pole holder at the wedding.

After the wedding, the new couple flew to London as planned, picked up Alan's car, and drove to Southampton to retrieve Joyce's trousseau from where it was being held in bonded storage, and then walk it through customs. Then they were off to Ilfracombe on the Devon coast to start their honeymoon. The morning after their romantic moonlit stroll by the sea, Joyce came down with the flu, and just as she began to recover, it was Alan's turn. So they packed it up and headed home to London to begin their lives together a week early. Joyce got a job as a teacher. But what a traumatic beginning to a marriage—grieving deeply for a beloved parent. Alan was a stalwart partner and learned to be a caregiver. Joyce took the necessary time to grieve, which offers its own path of maturation.

Did their lives become less complicated? Well, no.

Chapter 5

CY'S EARLY TRAINING: 1968

S tanding behind their convictions came naturally to these two, and when it came to their child there was no question that they would raise Cy at home no matter the advice and concerns of family and friends, nor current convention of thought and practice.

In those days new mothers stayed in the hospital for a week to ten days, but Joyce stayed for twice that long. Joyce would only eat ice cream when she came home. By the beginning of May, Joyce's mom, Dora, had arrived to help out. Dora wanted to impose her will about the way of doing things. Joyce was not that malleable, and so they were somewhat at loggerheads. Alan acted as mediator.

Down syndrome is accompanied by a predictable set of possible disabilities. Cy was very young when he began getting colds every few weeks. Children with Down syndrome are prone to respiratory difficulties, but it seemed Cy was more prone than is typical.

Nonetheless, "he was a beautiful baby and he was so good"—the picture of the developing newborn. In a letter to his parents on May 5, Alan describes Cy in the following way: "The only 'peculiarities,' if you could call them so, are his long and rather attractive eyes and his funny little ears . . . he is surprisingly strong and active, and can already roll from his side onto his back while being firmly tucked in." Like the education of any other child, stimulating Cy to become aware and curious about the surroundings and people in his world and helping him to learn skills began early.

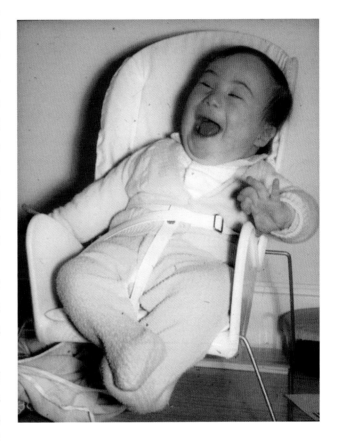

Joyce was a born teacher with the gifts of patience, high expectation for focus, and a can-do attitude. So it's no surprise that she began labeling the household when Cy was a just a newborn. She hung up little signs all around: "Door," "Mirror," "Bed." She spoke to Cy about the objects, requiring him to first make eye contact with her—"Look at me. Look at me"—and then pointing and guiding his focus to *Door.* So, though tiny, he was constantly hearing conversation, being directed to take in information and to follow instruction. Joyce's innate sense of the benefits of welcoming a child into his world with consistency and love would indeed eventually become the accepted pattern of stimulation for children with Down syndrome, though it would not be proven and become popular until decades later.

From the time Cy was a newborn baby, he used diapers, but later Joyce used to put him "on the potty" by holding him between her legs, and as he sat there, she talked about what he had to do in the toilet. It was a way of getting him used to "the required procedure" before he had his own little potty on which he could hoist himself up.

Chapter 6

DOCTOR'S RECOMMENDATION

After initially rejecting the idea of raising Cy at home, Alan's parents, Harry and Fanny, came to visit several months after he was born. Alan noted that they hadn't accepted Joyce easily into their family and didn't understand his love for her. Some adjustments were going to be necessary, as the family was bound to grow.

But witnessing Joyce mothering in action, and seeing the humanity in Cy won them over. They both grew to love her and Cy deeply. In fact, Joyce became the daughter Fanny never had, and Joyce took to Fanny in a way not possible with her own more hard-edged mother. Later on, the Brigishes and Dora would make annual trips to visit the family, staggering their visits.

As a result of the chromosome tests Alan and Joyce had taken, Joyce's doctor told them that the incidence of Joyce giving birth to another "baby like your first" carried only a "slight additional risk"; he proclaimed that the couple had "normal" DNA. He recommended that Joyce get pregnant again right away and insisted that she have an amniocentesis. She said she would refuse it. He was adamant. "Yes, you are going to have it," he said. "You don't want to have another Downs kid."

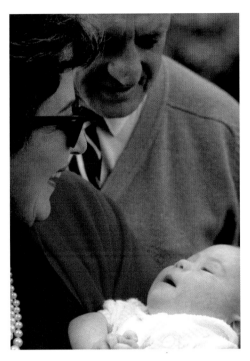

The couple didn't think they'd get pregnant again quite so fast. But they did, and the family was indeed going to grow. As Alan and Joyce were concerned about the risks associated with amniocentesis (which was a very new procedure at the time) and because they were very young and the tests they'd taken after Cy's birth had proved that his chromosome anomaly was not genetic, Joyce did not have the test to see whether the next baby had Down syndrome. Rather, they looked forward to the new addition to the family.

Hal was born in September of 1969. His birth was minimally easier than Cy's, but lengthy nonetheless.

Taking care of a newborn and a seventeen-month-old with a serious disability would be daunting for anyone. But part of loving babies is to keep them to a schedule, offering consistency. Joyce said, about the English, "They had a real thing about your babies being potty trained by the time they're eighteen months.[2] Cy had "no delays—in fact, he was ahead of the 'normal' person." Cy could sit up by himself by the summer of 1969, but he was unable to crawl and walking would be delayed for quite a while. Nonetheless, close friend Eileen Shaw remembers that Joyce had Cy potty trained during the day by the time Hal was born so that she would not have two lots of diapers. Cy had had ample time to learn to scoot up on to his own child-sized amenities.

In England, when he was two Cy went to a preschool that was part of the special needs agency. This gave Joyce some time alone with the baby. Cy was young, but very well-behaved, though not speaking much yet. The other children were speaking less than he was.

---

2 At the time it was quite the same in America, though, for some reason, the contemporary expectation for potty training is much later.

Chapter 7

MOVING AND MISCHIEF
CANADA & USA
1970

Alan had applied for a job with a U.S.-based start-up—one of the earliest online information companies—that was looking to rapidly expand into England. So the company sent Alan to the U.S. for training with others he'd recruited. A few weeks later the company's change in plan provided Alan with a choice: return to England with three months' severance pay or, with some of the people he'd brought with him for training, start up a business in Canada for the company.

Sometime previously, Alan and Joyce had serendipitously mused about maybe moving to Canada someday to see what life was like there, so Alan chose Canada. Alan returned to England for a week and the family made the move to Toronto, where their tenure was a horrendous experience for Joyce because Alan constantly needed to travel while she took care of Cy and Hal, neither of whom was walking yet. Also, their new neighbors in North America were not accepting of Down syndrome children. Joyce had a difficult time socially, and raising two little ones in a new city in a new country was demanding.

On a day trip to Niagara Falls, the four had a picnic. Two-year-olds have earned some notoriety and Cy was a typical two-year-old. All the family recalls him attempting to conk baby brother Hal over the noggin with a plastic hammer. True to form, Alan caught it on film.

1970 Connecticut—1st Time—
Stamford Mischief Makers

Five months later, Alan's company transferred him to Connecticut, and Joyce found an apartment in Stamford. Joyce again made the move with the two babies. One can only guess what strain moving house twice in such a short period of time put on them. But they were young and resilient.

And it's a good thing they were. Cy had difficulties with sleep. His sleeplessness had begun in England and continued when the family moved to Stamford in 1970 and would continue through 1971. Joyce said, "We used to take turns in his bedroom at night, because he couldn't sleep. One of us would sit on the floor next to his bed with an arm over him to keep him still and quiet and safe, and the other one would sleep for the next couple of hours, and then we'd switch. Eventually Cy learned to sleep at night, but it took a long time."

Cy was frequently admitted to the hospital with respiratory difficulties. Joyce could always rely on one of the friendly young mothers who lived in the same apartment building to look after Hal when she had to take Cy to the hospital.

Cy, The Fearless Wanderer

Still unable to crawl, Cy shuffled on his bum, pulling himself backwards with his hands and feet. Though these skills developed slowly, he could nonetheless mobilize at quite a clip. One day, two-year-old Cy went missing from the apartment. When Joyce and Alan discovered he was gone, they were beside themselves with worry as their fourth-floor apartment had a balcony. Wayward toddlers enjoy a boundless curiosity and an uncanny ability to slip away at great velocity in an unguarded moment. The hallway door must not have been completely closed and the elevator doors open. Cy scooted in, and in a timely fashion, someone called the elevator to the top floor. The doors shut and up he went, to be found by a worker on his way to the roof.

When called by the building superintendent, they admitted, yes, they were missing a child. The little guy had taken quite a long journey, and when they retrieved him, it had obviously been an untidy one. Cy was filthy. But, of course, though he had no way of letting on, he'd been bitten by the travel bug.

Most children are engaged by the constancy of gravity. Cy took great pleasure in throwing his Fisher-Price toys over the edge of that fourth-floor balcony with the hopes of hitting some car or something. One day, he disappeared again. His parents looked everywhere for him. The apartment doors were secure, so he hadn't gone upstairs, nor out to the balcony. Perplexed, they stood in the living room considering where to look next, when they heard him laughing and laughing. They found him in their bedroom closet, delightedly flinging shoes. He's always enjoyed throwing things, and to this day, a trip to the dump with Alan offers an opportunity for yet more joy in hurling things into the ether, always accompanied by a devilish laugh.

Shortly after the family moved, all four made a trip to buy furniture in a Sears Roebuck store in a dicey part of a nearby city. Hal was pushing Cy around in the stroller. One minute two boys were there, the next there was one. When shopping, both Alan and Joyce kept an eye on Cy, but they must have become distracted, because in a flash he was out of the stroller and off on an adventure, shuffling along on his bum.

Though there was a significant police presence in the store, Cy was not to be found. His parents were frantic and a number of people were looking for him. Somehow he'd gotten out of the store and was seen by a policeman, who brought him inside. All in all, the whole episode took perhaps fifteen or twenty minutes. Alan and Joyce were seriously alarmed as the policeman threatened to charge them with neglect, making for a very tense few minutes.

Because Cy doesn't enjoy hearing stories about his own mischief as a child, Joyce instead told stories about herself when she was small.

Joyce's parents (who were Jewish) had wanted her to learn about other religions, so they enrolled her in a Church of England convent school that she loved. She went to religious school for Jewish religious instruction, but she also went to mass, which wasn't required of her because she wasn't Catholic. Nonetheless, she enjoyed the ritual and learning about others' practices.

Eventually her parents had financial difficulties which required them to move to another town. She had to transfer from the convent school to a girls' boarding school. What Joyce thought of the boarding school was "I hated it, hated it, hated it."

So she made a plan.

She gave money to a day student to go to a store where they kept live rats. The shopping trip was successful and her friend carried a white rat to school nestled in a little box. The next evening Joyce snuck into the matron's room and put the rat in the matron's bed. Not saying a word, Joyce joined her friends who lived in the room just below. Soon enough there was a great deal of shrieking from above. The students were questioned and the matron pointedly asked Joyce if she was responsible. She owned up to it, knowing she'd get expelled. She was sent home and from then on she attended the school in the small town where her parents had moved, and there she was as happy as could be.

Apparently Joyce had also misbehaved at the convent school, but had so loved the nuns and her life there that she'd never admitted to being the clever designer of shenanigans that she was.

Cy's mischievousness has maternal roots.

Chapter 8

NEVER A DULL MOMENT & YET ANOTHER MOVE
USA – 1971

No matter what she was doing, Joyce tried to keep an eye on Cy, noting his whereabouts, what he was doing, and whether or not there were signals coming from him.

At three, Cy enjoyed piecing together his wooden jigsaw puzzles and could assemble them easily. At some point Joyce noticed that he couldn't do them anymore—and when he couldn't, he'd bang his head with his hands, or bang his head on the wall. Around the same time, she noticed that when he watched television, he was sitting right up in front of the set. And then he would bang his head. She sensed that his vision was diminishing for some reason. As Cy had not yet developed any language, banging his head in frustration was the signal that something was very wrong. Family friend Judy Machanik recalled that Joyce unconsciously understood Cy's signals. "It was an instinctive, responsible reaction to him," she said. "It was amazing to watch, and it was always present."

Joyce asked Cy's pediatrician to refer them to an eye specialist And the pediatrician said, "Don't waste your time. He'll be fine."

She listened to him. But when things hadn't improved after a week, she went back to the pediatrician and said, "I really don't want you to be concerned about my time and how much I waste it. I'd like the name of a specialist."

Alan was out of town on business. So, after settling Hal in with a neighbor, Joyce took Cy to an ophthalmologist. The diagnosis was that Cy had very dense cataracts in both eyes, with no vision in one and 70 percent cloudiness in the other, leaving literally only 20 to 30 percent vision remaining.

The doctor told Joyce not to worry about it. He added that because Cy was a "Downs person," he wouldn't need his eyes because he was never going to learn to read or write.

The doctor's telling Joyce that her child's condition made the quality of his future inconsequential surely did not put him in her good graces. As Joyce was very young, she didn't take him on, as a more mature Joyce would have later on. Instead, she and Alan did some research to find out where they would receive a more compassionate response.

The surgery to remove the cataracts was performed successfully at Boston Children's Hospital. As this occurred long before the advent of contemporary advances, the cataracts were literally cut out of his eyes, hoping for functional vision.

Because Cy had to be prevented from touching his eyes after the surgery, the doctors put his arms in splints and wrapped them. So he had to be fed. Down syndrome people are often double-jointed. Thus, Cy was able to somehow release his shoulder from the splint, and with his straight arm, he could reach his mouth. Typically, he'd fall asleep sitting up and then just flop forward and sleep on his legs.

As Cy is now considered legally blind and wears glasses with thick lenses, it's very possible that he would not have been able to see at all had he not had those surgeries.

Basil

Joyce had had birds as pets when she was a child. And when her own children were little, she had a parakeet named Basil (delightfully pronounced Bah'zil).

Basil was not confined to a cage but allowed to fly free in the kitchen, where he nibbled at the edges of the poster on the wall. When Joyce walked to Bloomingdale's from their apartment building, the babies in their double carriage, Basil came too. The fact that Basil was trained to ride on her shoulder even out of doors and that Bloomingdale's (a very fancy store at the time) allowed the untethered bird in the store proves that Joyce must have been adorable.

1972 Move Back to England

The family moved back to England again in 1972 when Cy was four and Hal was two and a half, during what Alan calls "a crazy period in our lives." Most of that burden of moving was shouldered by Joyce. Alan didn't have the time that was necessary because in 1970 he had joined National CSS (one of the pioneers of what is today known as cloud-based internet services) eighteen months after they'd launched in Stamford.

His new job (and the reason for the move) was to expand online services into the European market, starting in London. Alan was responsible for launching the data services business via a transatlantic cable. National CSS was the second company in the world to do so, GE having preceded them by weeks.

Alan's office was in London. But they lived in a bedroom community on the very edge of London's Green Belt, and he had an hour-long commute to and from London by subway (the tube) each day. He was also frequently traveling to Paris and Bonn, and also back to Stamford.

Hal and Cy

Hal and Cy (who were born just 17 months apart) have always been very close and they shared a room with bunk beds for a long time. Hal was always very helpful with Cy, even when he was very young himself.

At Cy's fourth birthday party, shortly before he learned to walk, Hal (who was two and a half) welcomed each guest at the door. He would then bring the present to Cy and help him open it.

Family friend Susan Grunthal recalled that when she met the Brigishes in 1972, Cy was walking at four and a half. She spoke of an instance where "some children were teasing Cy. Hal didn't like it if Cy was teased and got very upset. He became Cy's protector at quite an early age."

Chapter 9

INFLUENCING PUBLIC REACTION TO CY AND UNDERSTANDING HOW WE LEARN

Confronted with the time-consuming *daily* challenges of raising a child with disabilities, many might not have time to consider the future. But Joyce was all too aware of the cruelty that exists.

People experience a spectrum of reactions to those whom they perceive as different: sometimes it's from fear, or inexperience, or being ignorant of the fact that we are all human in spite of the variety of obvious attributes in which we are cloaked. Until we each understand that we are all human, ample opportunities for learning just that will present themselves.

Judy Machanik noted that "people would look at Cy and call him names, because of what they surmised about his intelligence. No one ever thought about the fact that there was a sensitive human being in there. And that name-calling and those kinds of things were going to have a deep effect."

When people stared at Cy and called him "retard," it cut Joyce deeply, incensed her, and heightened her determination.

Joyce hadn't wanted people to poke fun at Cy—then, or in the future—and she wanted to ensure that he wasn't singled out or ridiculed. Considering the climate of the time and the lens through which people with disabilities were viewed, this was one tall order. Nonetheless, from the very beginning, she had the long view about Cy's education and socialization. This surely was a harbinger for her work later in life, though it's unknown whether she perceived it at that point. As they had recently moved, she was yet again faced with what would become a lifetime's dedication to introducing Cy to a new community and a new community to Cy. As usual, Joyce's natural inclinations kicked in. She would teach him the social graces, to be polite and considerate of others. She intended that he be included in every aspect of family life and social gatherings and celebrations.

Joyce recalled a time when a girl threw sand in Cy's face and her parents said nothing. "And I had to say to the parents, 'You know, maybe you need to teach your daughter what the acceptable behavior is, and not allow her to do things like this. It's very hurtful, and it doesn't help your daughter, either.' They were apologetic and went off to speak to their daughter."

Judy Machanik noted that Joyce taught Cy to be polite and to "understand the value of courtesy. Joyce said, "He never knew to fight back . . . to give them what they'd given him. He would possibly come to one of us and say, 'That wasn't nice.'"

Judy said that Cy "was encouraged from an early stage . . . to be included in the conversation, and to be approved when it was appropriate, or disapproved when it was appropriate, which was very seldom—because misbehavior was not one of the things that he did." The key here is that he may never have known how (or chosen) to respond in kind to churlish or malicious comments, but he did learn to recognize the difference between acceptable and hurtful behavior.

Witnessing one's child on the receiving end of mindless or intentional cruelty can indeed evoke a Mother Bear reaction. The pain of that is something that requires processing so a parent doesn't get eaten alive by such senseless infringements. No matter how deeply they may have affected her, Joyce channeled those events into action for the benefit of positive change and to educate and raise the awareness of everyone she met.

Together she and Cy were a pair of ambassadors for compassion.

Cy attended a preschool that included mainly Down syndrome children. Witnessing what others were *not* doing to improve the children's patterns of speech and behavior, Joyce was adamant that she and Cy develop a relationship wherein Cy recognized that his mother expected no less from him than she would from anyone else. She tried to encourage other parents to join her in that endeavor, but was not successful getting them on board. Other households may not have had the advantages their family had (where time and resources were not an issue), but the *underlying* challenge, really, was to change an historical way of thinking. One of the key points in cultivating appropriate behavior is consistency, which requires that both parent and child resolve to always abide by the family's established guidelines for behavior, or to be called on it when behavior slips. As my storytelling friend Elizabeth Ellis used to say while raising her grandson (who was not disabled), "Good manners means constant vigilance." Her delivery with closed eyes, raised eyebrows, a slight shake of the head, and a tiny smile made me chuckle. But is it not the truth?

On Parenting

Though birthing classes have become an accepted part of our culture's preparation for the arrival of a new member of the family, parenting classes, on the other hand, have been extremely rare. Currently, more opportunities are available, and a number of books have been written to provide tools and support for parents raising children with disabilities—children who will one day be siblings, playmates, classmates, citizens, co-workers, employees, employers, leaders, volunteers, healers.[3] But at the time that Cy was born, the general practice was not to offer help, but to marginalize.

Joyce was a natural parent—gifted, some might say, and she had been trained as a teacher. So she understood the necessity of introduction, demonstration, explanation, repetition, and opportunity to practice any new skill.

She knew a child with Down syndrome would have developmental delays,[4] that it would take longer for Cy to develop his fine motor skills (which all children develop)—to learn to grasp and then use a crayon, pencil, paintbrush, or pen—than someone without such a disability.[5] She was sure he could learn those skills, so necessary in learning to print and write, color and draw or paint, but at a different rate of accomplishment. In the meantime, learning to sing the alphabet song and to recognize colors and geometric shapes, and the shapes of letters and numerals, would prepare Cy for the day when he could securely and adeptly hold implements of writing or other artistic expressions.

At least seven things are necessary for this: time, determination, trust,

---

3 10 Parent-Approved Books for Parenting Kids with Disabilities https://themighty.com/2017/08/disability-parenting-book-recommendations/

4 For readers who would appreciate a definition, it follows. Others, please indulge me. A developmental delay refers to a timeline of learning—not that the person is incapable of learning a skill, but rather that mastering the new capability will require more time and repetition for a person with developmental delays than is expected of a person without. Not only will it probably take longer to master that skill and add it to one's skill set, but the skills required as precursors for the new ability will also have taken longer to achieve and become consistently available to the learner.

5 A recent review in the Journal of Behavioral and Developmental Pediatrics, "Fine Motor Skills for Children with Down Syndrome: A Guide for Parents and Professionals" by Lucarelli, Jennifer MD; Davidson, Emily Jean MD, MPH, offers lists "of household objects and toys for skill development" https://journals.lww.com/jrnldbp/Fulltext/2017/04000/Fine_Motor_Skills_for_Children_with_Down_Syndrome_.12.aspx

patience, understanding, opportunity, and the willingness to take risks—exactly the same for any learner of any capacity, only in larger quantities. Joyce was aware that those qualities are equally crucial. A teacher offers moral support and sometimes physical support as well. And a very effective teacher offers the learner the opportunity to establish and reach a sequence of attainable goals that will result in building new skills. Joyce was blessed with a never-diminishing determination to see the tasks through and the time necessary to dedicate to a child with delays.

Joyce set small incremental and attainable goals so that the new skill wouldn't seem so overwhelming as to appear unattainable—and that is key: setting small goals helps minimize frustration. This also offers the opportunity for the *active repetition* which is the root of much learning. Being shown how to do something is often necessary, and having the opportunity to do it repeatedly oneself is what locks it into cellular memory and allows a skill to become part of one's repertoire. The skill is considered learned when it becomes second nature, or requires infrequent review.

Goal setting is a practice and a life skill and Joyce inherently knew that these would be the foundation of Cy's learning of all sorts of things. Of course, Cy would have limitations, but she hoped incremental goals and accomplishments would foster his determination to succeed, which in celebrating his success at achieving would foster his ability to take pride in his accomplishments and, further, to congratulate others.

Turns out, Cy *inherited* his mother's determination and applied it accordingly, though, like any child, he sometimes would have preferred to just play.

And patience? That's a challenge for most of us living in a culture that has developed an unreasonable expectation for immediate gratification. Luckily, Joyce had an abundance of it.

She also granted herself the time for a creative outlet—a satisfying way of keeping balance in a hectic life—and Joyce's medium was clay. She explained, "As English children go to school quite early, they have their dinner, which is tea, at about four o'clock, and they're ready for bed around five thirty, six. So, I did a lot of my pottery at night."

Chapter 10

FRIENDS

Judy Machanik glows when she talks about how Cy was brought along "with such enormous support and humor and love and [an] absolutely unwavering, unconditional 'you can do it.'"

The Machaniks, Judy and Jack, and the Hirshovitz families had been friends in South Africa. Joyce's mother, Dora, while visiting her daughter when they were living in the United States reintroduced Joyce to Jack Machanik, who was her brother Ivan's close friend. Judy, Jack, Joyce, and Alan established a friendship immediate and strong. When the Brigishes were once again living in England, the Machaniks visited.

Signals and School

Hal was attending preschool and Cy entered the "reception class" at the Breakspeare School in Watford on January 8, 1973, at age four and a half. When they returned from their day, they could each have two cookies, one for each hand; no more.

By then Joyce had developed some simple signals to alert Cy that he needed to modify his behavior. Some signals were visual and others auditory, which means that the two were in constant communication on some level; rare is that, and quite extraordinary.

To tell Cy that his hands were in the wrong place, Joyce would make a loose fist with her left hand and with her curved right palm tap the slight opening in the spiral of air made by the forefinger and thumb, making a sort of popping noise. He would hear it and know to move his hands. No one else would know anything about it.

If Cy's tongue pushed out of his mouth, she touched her finger to her bottom lip and he would know to pull his tongue back in. In spite of Cy's poor vision, mother and child were constantly aware of each other, and the relationship Joyce had wanted with Cy—so that he would understand that her expectations for him were no different than for anyone else—had indeed been established.

In school, as Cy came to feel more secure, he began to form relationships, a very good sign as he'd done everything in isolation. The headmistress at Breakspeare reported that when Cy first enrolled, he needed a lot of adult attention when confronted with new situations and was "withdrawn from group activity and from contact with other children." As he became more secure and developed relationships within the group, she described him as kind and thoughtful. Noteworthy is his independence when it came to self-care: "refusing all help" when it came to self-care.

Chapter 11

1974

ENTER . . . ONE
PRECIOUS BABY GIRL

Around the time that Alan had the honor of returning the favor of being a pole holder at Peter Grunthal's marriage to Susan on May 20, 1973, in Manchester, Joyce and Alan welcomed the confirmation that Joyce was pregnant. Jackie was born in February of 1974, after another lengthy labor. Joyce recalled how amazing Cy was with baby Jackie. Cy, almost six, "would take her for long walks in her carriage in England, up and down the road, to get her to sleep. Joyce said, "I don't think he ever left her side. You could get him to do anything with her."

The report from the school said quite plainly that Jackie's birth adversely affected Cy, that he was "stubborn, sulky, and withdrawn . . . refusing to talk about her or acknowledge her." This is the antithesis of what Joyce reports. Could it be that Cy was so attached to Jackie that he missed her when he went to school? Whatever the case, a later school report stated he was well integrated by the end of the summer.

Chapter 12

ACADEMIC PROGRESS AND A LITTLE MORE MISCHIEF

Ayear later, in the fall of 1975, when he was seven and a half, Cy transferred to "the first junior group," where he made steady progress. Notably he showed improvement in number concepts, opposites, shape and color recognition; he understood number value to 3 and could write 1, 2, and 3. From monosyllabic answers he had progressed to using sentences and holding conversations, even with adults unknown to him. So he was becoming less shy.

The arts had captivated Cy, and though he still worked in isolation, he enjoyed painting, movement, and drama.

Interestingly, a report from the psychiatrist who had been working with the family for two and a half years indicated that though Cy had been thought to be able to function in "the higher range of mental handicap," "he has proved over the years to be within the severely handicapped range." These results were based on observation and on test results.

Joyce said Cy generally acted more mature than he did during the testing sessions, in which the examiner described Cy as "friendly, persisting in a teasing, playful attitude." The test results were much lower than Joyce had expected and Cy was designated "in the severely subnormal range."

As Joyce said, "A lot of the Downs children have poor speech because their tongues thrust forward, getting in the way of eating and hindering enunciation. So we worked on it for years and years and years."[6] Joyce would remind Cy that his tongue had to stay in his mouth and not fall forward beyond his teeth. She said it was a matter of encouraging him to keep it in. The tongue is a strong and facile muscle, every part of it used for sound articulation. So Cy's speech was less thick and he learned to enunciate. Cy's hearing was fine, so he had no problem taking in correct pronunciation. Producing it was another matter, so he had speech therapy very early on, beginning in February of 1975.

The speech therapist reported that Cy made steady and great strides in their weekly sessions, in vocabulary, enunciation, concentration, and attention span. By June of 1976, with seventeen months of speech therapy behind him, he'd made enormous gains in controlling his tongue and in enunciation, the full articulation of multisyllabic words, and had abandoned his own vocabulary for the correct names for objects. He was successfully using verbs and adjectives, and his hyperactivity was decreasing as his interest and concentration increased, which allowed for a lengthening of his sessions to 40–45 minutes.

The therapist wrote that Cy was always pleasant and was beginning to classify objects, could "name most colors correctly and identify body parts and clothing . . . could count up to 12 meaningfully. His vocabulary has widened considerably and language is slowly developing."[7]

At the end of her report, she suggested that Cy, "with the correct

---

6 Describing people with Down syndrome, Dr. Down himself said, "They are usually able to speak; the speech is thick and indistinct, but may be improved very greatly by a well-directed scheme of tongue gymnastics." Quoted from a paper by Dr. John Langdon Down, for whom Down syndrome is named. http://www.downsyndromeprenataltesting.com/why-is-it-called-down-syndrome-or-why-i-wish-there-had-been-a-dr-awesome/

7 From a handwritten report dated June 10, 1976.

encouragement and stimulation, his stubborn determination can be used to help him achieve his full potential in all facets of speech and learning"—a much more promising and hopeful report than those of either the psychiatrist or the headmistress. It's quite clear that Cy responded well in a one-to-one learning situation and that his developmental delays were proving to be just that. All the strides he had made would be expected at a younger age in a child without his visual and intellectual disabilities. Nonetheless, he was progressing sequentially with all the necessary skills that are the precursors to reading and writing.

One can only imagine what a whirlwind of a household the Brigishes must have had at the time. Alan was working like a madman and had the hour-long commute each day, but was nonetheless making time to be with the family on weekends.

Hal and baby Jackie were blossoming. Outside of school, Cy was developing as any child would, according to his own abilities. Each year the family participated in the celebration of Guy Fawkes Day on November 5, an observance of gratitude that Mr. Fawkes's plan to blow up Parliament in 1605 had gone awry.[8] Bonfires and fireworks were enjoyed, and there were games and food. Cy particularly liked the booth with old china and wonderfully breakable things on the shelves. His love of throwing things was well indulged by the game which consisted of throwing a ball, the goal being to shatter the targeted dishware on the shelves.

His mischief making had not subsided as yet. The family lived in a house out in the country. One day Cy disappeared . . . again. He'd climbed into somebody's parked truck and, though he hadn't moved the truck, he was playing with the brakes when the owner got back from the store. Days later one of the neighbors' kids reported that Cy was playing in the neighbor's car. He did indeed release the brakes this time and the car rolled down the slight incline of the driveway and into the street. Neither Cy nor the car was injured and the owners were very decent about it. Hal recalls that "Cy would be giggling and laughing the whole time," suggesting it was not an isolated incident.

Having two young boys will keep any mama on her toes. These two were always into something. The day that Hal got the training wheels removed from his bike . . . Well, let's let him tell it: "I tried to ride down the driveway and bee-lined the bike into the rose hedges! Those things were evil! I got hurt pretty badly, had a scar going all the way up my front torso for many years, and a little one going across. No stitches though; Mom patched me up. No repercussions as far as I remember. The roses were fine.

---

8 Guy Fawkes Day: http://www.history.com/news/guy-fawkes-day-a-brief-history

I wanted to cut them down. You can bet I figured out how to ride pretty quickly after that."

Then, of course, there was the time Hal ate a mushroom—"a toadstool," he told the emergency room doctor. Whatever it was, he was treated and survived to tell the tale.

Chapter 13

GRANDPARENTS

Joyce's mother, Dora, came for a visit each year and learned to treat the three children the same way their parents did: no special dispensation for Cy. She came as often as she could and stayed a month.

Once the Brigishes moved permanently to the U.S., family reunions were every four years or so, either in South Africa, Connecticut, or somewhere in Europe. It was a big expense for them. Hal said, "I remember great times when they visited us and spent time on Martha's Vineyard, Mom and Dad would rent a house for a few weeks in the summer back then and we'd go to the beach, fly kites, and swim. My grandfather [Harry] loved swimming in the surf, or as he'd call them, 'the breakers.' Our grandmother [Fanny] would not swim, but enjoyed the time on the beach. Perhaps, she, like our mother, was worried about sharks.

"They were really fun times we had with them, both in SA, and in the U.S. My paternal grandparents were rebels. I grew to understand that and appreciate it. I liked the idea of questioning the norms. I really idolized them. My grandfather could be a real curmudgeon, but he was a very lovely man and really enjoyed being with us—our grandmother, too. I felt very close to them, despite the long distance.

"Unfortunately, we never met our maternal grandfather. We had plenty of stories from Mom, though. I really wished I could have met him. But Mom's mother [Dora] was terrific. When she came to visit us in Connecticut, she would somehow play baseball with me."

Because his parents treated the boys as equally as they could, Hal had a fresh viewpoint on the world. By example, he had learned to treat people the same. Joyce said, "Hal didn't see his brother as disabled, nor did he see his grandmother Dora, who had had one leg amputated, that way. She would travel to America on her own, and stay for about a month. Hal didn't hesitate to ask her to come outside and throw balls for him. Even before she was using a prosthesis, she would go outside, lean on her crutch, and throw balls for him, and he had an amazing relationship with her."

Hal continued: "She smoked cigarettes, which made my mother crazy." Joyce forbade her to smoke indoors. "If she ran out of cigarettes, she'd try to bribe me to ride my bicycle to the store which was four or five miles away on windy main roads with no shoulder. I would always refuse since I knew my mother would not approve. But I did feel bad as I knew she really wanted it. My grandmother was strictly kosher, and we were certainly not. But my mother was respectful enough, despite her rebellious ways, to keep only kosher meat in the house when her mother was visiting—or maybe she would somehow hide what was non-kosher."

Chapter 14

A SHOT AT PUTTING DOWN ROOTS

The children's birthdays were always multigenerational celebrations that would include several families each with three children. Cy enjoyed blowing out the candles, which became a lifelong delight. His eighth birthday was the last Cy would celebrate in England.

The family was about to make a permanent move to Weston, Connecticut, in 1976, with an arrival date of August 16. The plan was to take a family vacation first. Alan said, "It was a logistical nightmare, perfectly executed by Joyce with some help from me. We had to rent our house in England, ship our furniture to the USA, and drive to Marina di Pietrasanta in Italy, rent a villa, hang out for a few weeks on the beach while the furniture was being shipped (not a hardship), return to England, sell the car, deal with visas for the family—all while we were buying a house in Weston, and purchasing two cars in the USA—this with three kids. Jackie was two and a half. And I was transitioning from running an international outpost to going to a big corporate job."

At the end of the final transatlantic journey, the Machaniks met the five Brigishes at the airport—and so began decades of sharing holiday celebrations together—Passovers and Thanksgivings at Jack and Judy's and Christmases at Joyce and Alan's.

They arrived in Connecticut on a wing and a prayer, just in time to race around and get the children registered for school, and do the countless things one does to take up residence in a new house in a new town. Alan was off to the corporate world and the very capable Joyce was on deck to organize life in the States once again.

The boys made friends with the neighborhood kids and began an uninterrupted life of school, community, and play, and the family settled in. The

intercontinental migration was over. Nonetheless, it's fair to say that this sort of geographical upheaval can set any child back a bit until the dust settles. The strong family unit and its constancy had always been a boon to them as they all adjusted to a new home and surroundings.

Both boys were used to doing chores—making their beds, helping with the dishes, taking out the garbage—and they had become quite adept socially—exactly what their parents would expect from all three children.

Come September, Hal entered second grade at Weston Elementary School, and Cy entered the Coleytown Developmental Center (CDC) in Westport where he became part of what the center described as "a small class for children with moderate mental retardation [receiving] instruction in pre-academic skills, social adaptation, pre-vocational skills, psychomotor skills, self-help skills, oral communication and practical skills. Also . . . support services in the areas of speech therapy, physical education, occupational therapy, music and art."[9] CDC had opened in 1974.[10]

Our world and the English language can be so very ambiguous. Clarity is a gift for both giver and receiver. Judy Machanik spoke about the clarity with which Alan and Joyce raised Cy, both being clear about values, what was "good and bad," how to respond politely in conversation, which helped him develop his ability to relate to the world, to people—family, friends, and strangers, "and by example, how he dealt with his siblings—from the time they were just little kids. They were just intuitive, and Joyce had this magical way of just making him feel comfortable and safe and accepted."

9 End of year report, May 2, 1978, Special Education Co-ordinator

10 Losen, Joyce. "Coleytown Staff Makes 'Mainstreaming' Work." *Westport News*, Wednesday, May 16, 1979.

Chapter 15

INTRODUCING A NEW NEIGHBORHOOD TO CY

Joyce had been an ocean swimmer as a child in South Africa, where the presence of sharks required that two nets be constructed across the entrance to the swimming area to protect swimmers. Once she was dragged by the undertow through a hole in the first shark net and had to be rescued. End result: "I don't like the ocean." But she was fine swimming in a pool.

Great news for the Brigish children when they moved to Weston was that their parents had a swimming pool installed in the back yard. Because Cy has minimal depth perception, he couldn't see well going into the pool and was nervous about the steps. The reflections on the water's surface made it difficult, so it took a while for the family to help Cy feel comfortable with the pool. But once in—well, the word "fish" comes to mind. The family made a game that Cy loved of diving to the bottom to pick up colored rings that were big enough to be visible.

Hal recalled that Cy would play for hours in the pool and eventually he became a really good swimmer, though he'd never had a lesson.

The Brigishes opened their backyard pool to their neighborhood. So there were often quite a few kids there. Joyce, of course, wouldn't be Joyce without a set of ground rules. If a flag was waving from the mailbox, it meant the family didn't want company. No flag, and the neighborhood was welcome to come join the fun—with one stipulation: "I told parents, 'Don't send your children without you being present, because I'm not babysitting.'" That way, there'd be enough supervision and the families could enjoy each other—and the kids could get used to being around Cy—one of the reasons for extending such a magnanimous invitation. Some neighbors didn't want to, so they just didn't join in.

Chapter 16

HEALTH, EDUCATION, AND WELFARE

1977

Cy had been such an active boy and Joyce made sure the family always ate healthy meals. Nonetheless, Cy continued to have respiratory problems and caught colds easily. In February of 1977 in Weston, when Cy was eight, Joyce and Alan were having a dinner party. Cy got very sick and was having trouble breathing. Joyce went up to check on him, and shouted for Alan as Cy had stopped breathing. Alan ran up the stairs in a panic, and then managed to fall down the stairs and sprain his ankle. He remained with Hal while Joyce rushed Cy to the hospital. On arrival, Cy was turning blue, and it was necessary to give him a tracheotomy to save his life. Nonetheless, Cy has a certain amount of natural resiliency. Alan recalled that the next day when he hobbled into the hospital on crutches to visit, Cy said, "Hi, Dad! Can I have a chocolate milkshake?"

The dramatic events of raising a child with multiple disabilities can take their toll on caregivers. Joyce knew the value of respite from responsibility, and she knew that artistic expression offers spirit-soothing engagement with a medium and with other artists. So, when Cy was

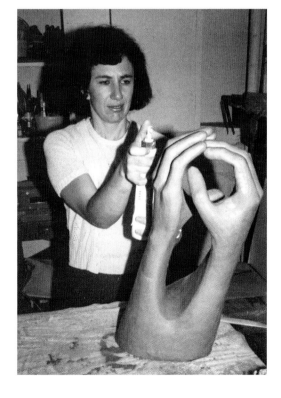

about nine, Joyce began studying sculpting with world-renowned sculptor Stanley Bleifeld, and would do so for more than a dozen years.[11]

One way or another, the whole family took some time out each summer to play at the beach.

44

Chapter 17

LATE 1970S
CHILDHOOD BIKES

Riding bikes was a favorite pastime. As the family lived on a dead-end road with a cul-de-sac, making for a low-traffic area, Hal and the neighborhood kids rode to the end and played whiffle ball and stickball. Cy, of course, joined them for those games or to watch them "jump bikes" on slanted boards they assembled, or to play backyard football or basketball at Hal's friends' houses. Cy got a three-wheeler when he was around ten.

Hal recalls that "Cy had some younger friends on the street who were his buddies and looked up to him for a bit while they were young and rode with him. They had a little gang. They knew he was 'different' but they seemed to have good times.

"I would be on my two-wheeler and kids in the neighborhood would have theirs, and he'd be on his big three-wheeler with a basket in the back. And sometimes we would sit in the basket and he would just ride us around. He's very strong. He would *ride* that thing. Cy was fearless.

"We'd go down to this one corner. He'd go as fast as he could—because he just knew the roads. He couldn't see it so well, but he knew where everything was, and he'd be going around the corner and he'd be up on two wheels. We had

another friend who had a skateboard. We would tie a rope to the back of Cy's trike and Cy would go down the hill pulling this kid on a skateboard. I'd be in the back. I can't believe we never had any major wreck."

Of course, their parents knew nothing of this. They were all growing up, riding together until adolescence pivoted their social itinerary.

Chapter 18

CELEBRATING ADVANCES AND NOT JUDGING THOSE WHO CAME BEFORE

Judy said that Alan and Joyce "were so committed to making sure that Cy had his place in the world, that he knew where he could go, what he could do, and his life was so enriched in so many ways—camp and friends and social events. There was always this inclusion for him, with everything—except misbehavior."

I think it's important at this juncture to say something about the velocity of change: it can seem glacial. With regard to Joyce's expectations of Cy, and what she knew in her heart to be true about human beings—well, she was just flat-out ahead of her time. In any era when strides have been made, it is, perhaps, difficult to refrain from judging those who came before for not "getting with the program" sooner, so that fewer people would have suffered and more would have benefited from a more progressive—even daring—way of thinking. That judgment can really be a waste of time unless we learn from it that while we're busy holding tight to our beliefs, the human race might indeed move forward at a smarter clip if we leave space open in our hearts and minds for the possibility of a leap of faith.

Joyce was asking—and would continue to ask—those around her to take that leap of faith and raise expectations for those so long marginalized, allowing them to at least explore their capabilities, potential, and parameters. What she was actually asking was for people to agree that what we share is

the desire and need and right *to belong*, and that if we have not been given the opportunity to try to attain our aspirations, we might not even be aware that we have the right to have them.

Often she was frustrated by those who beheld a vast terrain of possibilities, yet chose to tread a well-worn path. While Joyce may have felt she was the flag bearer of her own revolution, other like-minded change agents were making waves in other communities at the same time. Happily, she met and collaborated with those crusaders along the way, those who could sense and appreciate someone's spirit before tramping about in the conditional mundane. With that gift of camaraderie, they were unstoppable.

In neighboring Massachusetts a movement had been afoot to create a law that mandated education for *all* children. America's first special education law, Chapter 766 had been passed in 1972 and "served as the model for the first federal special education law, passed in 1975,"[12] which provided education until age twenty-one, specifically "free, appropriate" education "in the least restrictive" environment. In this day and age, it may be difficult to

---

12 https://massadvocates.org/history/ Massachusetts law Chapter 766 was instituted in 1972.

imagine what it was like for families whose children were excluded from public education. But that was exactly the scenario that prompted the movement for inclusion in Massachusetts.[13]

Joyce lived and breathed advocacy for inclusion and fought long and hard in the beginning to get people's attention, and then, following that, to raise their awareness and then to implement change. She innately understood that the similarities and differences of the human family are more accurately depicted as a Gordian knot rather than as columns on a spreadsheet. Such is the nature of the variety of disabilities. She championed the individual program for each child, and strived to help people understand that a vital part of the education of us all was in the collective interplay of the communities of students, that getting to know each other would further understanding, acceptance, and, dare we say it, a celebration of our differences through the discovery of our similarities.

A May 1978 *Wall Street Journal* article cited Edwin W. Martin, deputy U.S. education commissioner for the handicapped, on educational practices that predated the federal law. "Even when a school district had a handicap program, he says, it often lumped together students with all sorts of physical, mental and emotional disabilities. 'Kids were being segregated for administrative purposes, not for educational reasons.'"[14]

Instituting those improvements in the education of all children takes time and planning. The *Westport News* featured an informative article in 1978, "Handicapped Look to Future," by Ti'maun Southworth. The CDC (Coleytown Developmental Center), part of the Westport school system, served children with special needs in a large region of Fairfield County. Needs of children with disabilities (minimal or extreme, and generally different disabilities) that set children apart could not always be met in a public school system, and the CDC was a viable alternative for families. The Steering Committee for Special Education (in its third year in 1978 and affiliated with the Parent Teacher Association of CDC), comprising parents of such

---

13 Ibid.

14 Jaroslovsky, Rich. "Can You Educate Handicapped Kids at Regular School?" *Wall Street Journal*, Thursday, May 11, 1978.

children was making headway, especially since the enactment of the U. S. law which not only raised awareness nationwide, but made it mandatory that parents be involved in developing the education programs for their children with special needs.

The steering committee "works with the school to develop programs . . . and is also concerned with recreation, jobs and housing . . . and with the lives of other members of special ed families."

The coordinators of the steering committee, Skip Carey and Linda Lustig, explained the focus of their group. Ms. Lustig said, "Even if a parent recognizes the nature of their child's problem, they may try to push him to be as normal as possible instead of allowing the child to learn what he can do best."

At the time, all involved had the long view. Southworth wrote, "One of their long-range goals is complete acceptance of their children by the community, an acceptance that would include future employment and independence within the community as the children grow up."

There wasn't an abundance of work opportunities at the time, but it was hoped that when employers saw the capabilities of the young adults, they'd be more apt to hire them. "Depending on ability level and with vocational training, many kids should be able to work in restaurants, care for animals, do office work and provide services for older people," Carey said.

Co-operative housing overseen by parents was also in the offing. "We want to get away from institutions as much as possible and keep the kids near home." Ms. Lustig said. "The burden gets heavier on a family once the child has grown and graduated." [15]

Alan and Joyce were deeply involved in every aspect of Cy's life, and when advocating for Cy, they, like the reported "twenty active leaders and over one hundred members" of the Steering Committee for Special Education[16] were advocating for changes for *all* families with children with special needs.

The school's focus, understandably, was on moving forward with improvements in the quality of education. In addition, the Brigishes were concerned with the quantity and quality of the communication, that it include them in every step of the process of programming for Cy. A series of letters went back and forth between Alan and Joyce and the administration to that end. And of course, Joyce was adamant that the whole student population be involved in some sort of awareness program.

I was a public school teacher in the late 1970s in Massachusetts, where

———————————

15 Southworth, Ti'maun. "Handicapped Look to Future." *Westport News*, August 30, 1978.

16 Ibid.

mainstreaming had become mandatory when Chapter 766 was passed in 1972 and the federal law in 1975. The changes were afoot and they took some time to implement. I recall that for some it was a difficult sell because people could anticipate that there would be a need for additional personnel, supplies, and possibly facilities, which meant budget concerns. Others had greeted the realities of mainstreaming with trepidation, and some considered it an experiment of sorts, not really believing it could work, but willing, of course, to make the necessary adjustments. On the other hand, the champions of inclusion were so grateful for changes in expectations, and leaned into the possibilities with great anticipation. Proponents of a "wait and see" attitude as well as those in every camp had to admit, in the end, that mainstreaming and inclusion provided growth and benefits for us all. Additionally, the expanding nature of the school community more realistically represented the greater community, as we actually experienced the changing reality of who is entitled to an education in America.

As always, Joyce was perpetually aware of the need for Cy to learn acceptable behavior. She wasn't the only one who held her child to a standard. In a 1979 news article about the Coleytown Elementary and Junior High School's success at mainstreaming (which was still a relatively new educational concept), Dr. Christianson of that school system praised the efforts of the staffs at both schools in meeting the challenges of incorporating children with intellectual, physical, and emotional disabilities into their classrooms. With respect to behavior, he had a wonderfully down-to-earth, honest response. The article's author wrote, "Lest one assume that normal children have exclusive rights to 'difficult' behavior and that children in wheelchairs are necessarily docile and well-behaved, Dr. Christianson set the record straight. 'Children with handicaps come in the same behavioral varieties as normal children,' he said, 'and we have had experience with "hellraisers" on wheels who could give any normal child stiff competition. For the most part, discipline problems are dealt with in the same way for handicapped children as for normal children. Among the values of mainstreaming is that children learn that they will be measured by the same standards as everybody else.'" [17]

In May 1978, after two years at the CDC, Cy was ten years old. The end-of-year report from the Special Education Coordinator painted a more hopeful picture than the one drawn several years previous.

Joyce and Alan remained stalwart advocates for Cy's education, attending meetings and writing letters. Parents were making a very serious difference in the quality of the education for their children with special needs.

---

17 Losen, Joyce. "Coleytown Staff Makes 'Mainstreaming' Work." *Westport News,* Wednesday, May 16, 1979.

Chapter 19

CY'S FIRST
SPECIAL OLYMPICS

Joyce and Alan wanted to get Cy more involved in the community. The Coleytown Development Center sponsored Special Olympics[18] for its students, and his parents thought Cy might enjoy it and that it would help keep him fit. When they explained it to Cy, at first he said he couldn't run, he couldn't do high jump, or anything at all. His participation would require a change in attitude. Joyce said, "Eventually we taught him the expression 'Yes, I can, sir,' and he began training with his schoolmates at the Westport Y. His motto became 'Yes, I can.'"

Held on June 3 and 4, 1978, the Connecticut Special Olympics[19] (which had begun in 1968) showcased 1,500 athletes and 2,000 volunteers. That was Cy's first experience at the event, and along with a number of other track and field events, he would run the 50-yard dash. Because of his poor vision, standing at the starting line, he couldn't see the finish line. So Alan, Joyce, Hal, and four-year-old Jackie ran next to him, shouting, "Yes, you can! Yes, you can!" and he came in fourth. Eventually he would progress to the 100-yard and 200-yard dashes.

A special treat for the competitors was the appearance of a passel of Disney characters that came to Special Olympics to encourage the runners. The "Yes, I can" motto fell flat with this one because Cy was petrified of them, so the family had to keep them away.

---

18 From the Special Olympics website: "Special Olympics is a global movement of people creating a new world of inclusion and community, where every single person is accepted and welcomed, regardless of ability or disability. We are helping to make the world a better, healthier and more joyful place—one athlete, one volunteer, one family member at a time." https://www.specialolympics.org/Sections/Who_We_Are/Who_We_Are.aspx?src=navwho

19 http://www.soct.org/

Special Olympics has a motto as well: "Let me win, but if I cannot win, let me be brave in the attempt." And medals are awarded: "for skill, for courage, for sharing, and for joy."[20] Cy received his first medal—a bronze—for placing third in the long jump. To say the boy was pleased doesn't even come close.

Included in the standings: Cy, 11 years; 4th place in 50-yard dash, softball throw, and 440-yard junior relay; 3rd place, long jump. Cy was in good and familiar company as four mates from Coleytown—Sue Taylor, 16; Doug Price, 11; Michael Brasslett, 12; and Jesse Lustig, 14—also won gold, silver, and bronze medals in a variety of events.[21]

"Yes, I can!" had a long reach, becoming the motto for reading and for the study of other skills for the following decades. And, of course, it didn't take Joyce long to become deeply involved with Special Olympics.

The following year, a news article described the origins of area involvement in Special Olympics. The team had begun with only six athletes, and four years later (1979), they would boast twenty-five 8-to-21-year-olds. Geri Price and Joan Wyatt were co-chairs for the area and mothers of two of the team members.

According to *Weston Voice* writer Jack Betteridge, "When they started, Price said, they were a disheveled crew with no uniforms and an old sheet for a banner in the Olympic parade. 'All these other teams looked like they'd just stepped out of a sporting goods store.'" A serious (and successful) effort was made to get the team uniforms.[22]

Geri Price, Linda Lustig, and Joyce went to the Community Services Advisory Council in early summer of 1979 seeking assistance for their recreation program at the Westport Y. "They said the weary mothers who had

---

20 Leslie Chess Feller received a first place award from the Connecticut Press Club for her article "Cy Brigish . . . Profile of a Special Olympian," November 19, 1987, in *The Weston Voice*, from which this quote is taken.

21 Paraphrased from the article, "Our Special Olympic Champs" from *The Weston Forum*, June 14-20, 1978.

22 Paraphrased from "Special Olympic is for Special People." by Jack Betteridge, *The Weston Forum*, June 22, 1979.

been helping for the past three years need replacements."[23] They requested two high school students with water safety instruction certificates to help (in paid positions) with the swimming program. The triad of change agents also requested transportation for people with disabilities and said they wanted "to establish an awards program for both participants and volunteers." Their requests were received favorably and council members said they would seek instructors and "funding from local organizations."

23 Laos, Katie. "Mothers Ask Town Help for Special Recreation Program." *Westport News,* Friday, June 29, 1979.

Chapter 20

1979

SUMMER JOY

T he family took a sojourn to Italy in the summer and, as usual, made sure they were seaside. For Cy, the summer of 1979 would be life-changing.

Camp Jabberwocky

In 1976, when the Brigishes first moved to Weston, Connecticut, Sue McBrinn, mother of Cy's classmate Patrick, told Joyce about Camp Jabberwocky, a summer camp on Martha's Vineyard for children with disabilities. Joyce asked about the application process and discovered that the campers are

there by invitation. As the family had only just arrived in America, Joyce got in touch with founder-administrator Helen Lamb to find out the specifics.[24] In Helen, Joyce found a kindred spirit.

In 1979 when he was eleven, Cy was invited to Camp Jabberwocky for one week. He loved it. The second year he was invited for two weeks, and then for three and then four weeks. Now he's grandfathered in for four weeks, whereas any new camper can be invited for a maximum of two weeks.

The first summer camp for the handicapped established in the United States, Camp Jabberwocky bears the name of Lewis Carroll's fantastical poem, and the campers' cabins' names are drawn from Carroll's invented words. Cy was assigned to "Mome Raths" his first summer and has lived there every August for all these years.

Helen Lamb's vision began the summer of 1953 and continues on as her stunning legacy of joy and acceptance. "The idea of camp is to stretch the muscles and the minds and the creativity of physically and mentally handicapped people, to get them out of the house, away from their families

24 Camp Jabberwocky began in 1953 at Happy Days, a cottage in the Martha's Vineyard Camp Meeting Association. The summer of 1954 it moved to the 4-H Club in Oak Bluffs on New York Avenue.

Hanjian, Clark. Camp Jabberwocky – A Brief History of the *Martha's Vineyard Cerebral Palsy Camp*. Martha's Vineyard Cerebral Palsy Camp, Vineyard Haven, MA. 1989.

and—once here—off the camp grounds, into the community and all over the Island. . . With no thought, they accept one another, no matter the age, no matter the degree of disability."[25]

In addition, no other discernible attribute separates them, either. Jabberwocky is a wellspring of integration and inclusion on every level, and to be among this extraordinary group of counselors—who work for free—and campers who wait all year long to return, one discovers a Brigadoon of sorts looming from the mist of our curious greater culture of separating out those

who are different—not once every hundred years, but for the much more satisfying schedule of every summer on the Vineyard since the camp's inception sixty-five years ago.

Camp Jabberwocky used to host adults in July and children in August,[26] though some of the adult longtime campers still attend in August due to capacity or tradition, and because when some young ones

---

25 Stout, Hilary. "Camp Jabberwocky Brings These Children Love, and Each Sunny Day, a Trip to the Beach." *Vineyard Gazette*, Friday, August 15, 1986. This article, with wonderful photographs, includes a substantial history of Camp Jabberwocky.

26 Camp Jabberwocky has recently added a third session for families at the end of the season.

became eligible to move to adult camp, they flat-out didn't want to make the move. Formerly, each session culminated in a "play,"[27] often a familiar film story or fairy tale, so fractured and funny that new audience members are often compelled to begin a summer tradition that very night. Audiences have just loved Camp Jabberwocky's wild renditions of "A Fisherman's Wife," "Snow White," "Oliver Twist," "Sherlock Holmes," "Beauty and the Beast," "Robin Hood," "Cinderella," "The Princess and the Pea," "Waiting for Godot," "The Magic Flute," "Labyrinth," "Star Wars," and "The Wizard of Oz," to name but a fraction of their creative endeavors.

Vineyard Gazette writer Tom Dunlop wrote: "Another reason to see a Jabberwocky musical is to watch the

---

27 Currently, the play schedule is variable.

players triumph over the accidents that befall them on stage. This is what the place is about, after all—the accident of cerebral palsy or Down syndrome or spina bifida strikes, and at Jabberwocky the individual spends his days doing more than the rest of the world ever expected—or sometimes permitted—him to do. When you put together a musical in about 20 hours of rehearsal

time, you get some doozies."[28] He goes on to relate how mistakes and accidents are taken in stride and dealt with—with panache.

One of the great joys of summer on the Vineyard is the appearance of the Jabberwocky campers wending around the corner onto Main Street or traipsing down North Water Street in the 4th of July parade in Edgartown, amidst fire trucks, the prom queen and her court, police officers, marching representatives of organizations, various clever political floats, our town and county leaders, our flag-bearing veterans in uniform, classic automobiles, and whoever can come up with and pull together an idea that will "float." For decades, the counselors and campers, dressed in an eclectic assortment of "party wear" and a huge array of costumes, hoot and holler and wave to the crowd to great applause as they pass, those who can walk doing so and some

28 Dunlop, Tom. "Young Campers of Jabberwocky End Summer with a Wild Snow White." *Vineyard Gazette*, August 29, 1995.

pushing their friends in wheelchairs. The bright red Camp Jabberwocky bus, an iconic image on the Island, transports others for whom the distance would be too great, the campers hanging out the windows to greet parade-goers. It's as if the party was all theirs, and Independence Day was an also-ran. Such unbridled joy is not to be missed.

Chapter 21

HERNIA SURGERY
THANKSGIVING 1979

The joys of Special Olympics and attending Camp Jabberwocky gave Cy new communities of inclusion and he relished participating in both. Enjoyment notwithstanding, Cy has had multiple medical problems his whole life, and they demanded regular attention in between the glories of sports and camp.

Cy has a high pain threshold. So when he complains, his family listens. The day before Thanksgiving, Cy had had hernia surgery, and the surgeon cleared him to travel by car with his family to their friends Jack and Judy Machanik's home for their traditional holiday get-together.

That evening Cy was doubled over in pain. They called the surgeon as they didn't know what to do. The doctor told them to ignore it as he was "only a Down syndrome person."

Everyone was furious, and Cy had no relief. They took him back to Connecticut the next day, this time to Yale, where there was a doctor who had treated Cy previously. He was taken back into surgery immediately. Inside Cy, the surgeon found that a sponge, the tip of a metal tool, and a length of surgical thread had been left behind after the initial surgery.

After two surgeries in such a short time, Cy was feeling miserable. But, resilient as ever, he made a good recovery. Unfortunately, it would be only the first of five hernia operations over the years.

The family decided against legal action. As Joyce said, "It was a small community. Cy needed doctors. And so we had to weigh out the situation." But she did confront the doctor. One can only imagine that encounter with an outraged Joyce.

CHAPTER 22

THE
PRONOUNCEMENT

T he 1980s continued with highs and lows. In other words, the lives of the Brigish family were never dull.

The world simply did not see Cy the way his family did. Judgments about who he was—and his worth in this world—traveled along the lines of the status quo, discounting his value and his potential. A parent informed Joyce that Cy had been pronounced not educable. The reasons for that pronouncement are unknown. A news reporter interviewing Joyce much later, wrote "told . . . that Cy would never be able to learn to read, write, or do math, Joyce admits that she 'threw a fit.'"[29] Her exact response: "Oh, don't you tell me that! You don't tell me that he's not educable." Joyce had the skills of patience and indefatigable determination. She knew that considering Cy uneducable was folly as she had al-

ready experienced years of his accomplishments proving the opposite. So she "withdrew him from the school program, and worked with him herself for

---

29 Feller, Leslie Chess. "Cy Brigish . . . Profile of a Special Olympian." *Weston Voice*, November 19, 1987.

a full year with results that proved his abilities beyond any doubt." [30] Joyce worked one-on-one with Cy each morning at home; he attended school in the afternoon for socialization.

Cy had learned so many things, including behaviors that would help with Cy's acceptance in any community; he'd learned the social graces, such as how to greet visitors at the door and to initiate conversation, asking about one's family—by name, as Cy has a very strong memory. He'd learned to appreciate and practice good hygiene, and his mother made sure he always wore clothes that had been well cared for. He had learned fine table manners (one can be sure Joyce made certain of that); and with his improved speech, he learned telephone etiquette. All this had taken time and practice, but as we know, these graces bring their own reward, as they are the social tools that we recognize as familiar. Whether we wish to believe it or not, how a person conducts him- or herself on first meeting and how his or her actions coincide (or not) with our own social values and rituals are, in great part, how we measure someone up.

When it came to academics, Joyce said, "Teaching him to read—well, it was stubbornness on my part. Because I was *not* going to be told that Cy was 'not educable.'"

The Bertins, Bill and Phyllis and children Mark and Rachel, had met the Brigishes in 1978 as neighbors and so had begun a deep friendship, the two families sharing life on many levels. As Mark said, "The Brigishes were not just neighbors. They were 'family.'"

Phyllis was a teacher and knew a great deal about teaching reading to children with special needs. Joyce was eager to learn. So Phyllis and Joyce had

---

30 Ibid.

many discussions about how to teach beginning reading. Joyce then adapted what she had learned to fit Cy's specific needs. He progressed, and as with any reading student, the true test was comprehension and retention. So, they stuck with some of the lower-level books, and retention was apparent.

Cy eventually achieved about a fourth-grade reading level. Even now, Cy enjoys reading the headlines of the newspaper. He might struggle a bit over some of the words, but someone will step in to help. Joyce said, "Because his vision is so poor, he can't read small print. But he'll read the headlines. And he'll say, "Oh, look, Dad. There's a story about Obama!"

As Phyllis said, "With a great deal of patience and intelligence she accomplished what no one else thought could be done."

Joyce added: "And of course *Sesame Street*[31] played a big role in helping. I was just so determined to get him to read and write."

---

31 The acclaimed children's television program, *Sesame Street* launched November 10, 1969, which makes it nearly as old as Cy!

Chapter 23

ALWAYS BUSY
LEARNING SOMETHING

It wasn't all hard work, though. August found Cy back at his beloved Camp Jabberwocky, and Joyce and Alan took Jackie and Hal to the island as well. Joyce recalled this delightful moment: "Before we owned a house, I would stay at a hotel in Vineyard Haven. One time I went to a beach—I didn't realize it was the Jabberwocky beach." Joyce dozed off in the sun and the campers arrived at the beach while Joyce was sleeping.

"I woke to this voice that I knew too well. Cy had planted himself right there," she said, pointing a foot away from her, "and he didn't see me. He hadn't seen me in weeks. When he discovered me, he flipped—introduced me to all his new counselors."

And while it might seem the family's world revolved around Cy, it wasn't so. Big things were happening and Joyce and Alan's commitment to supporting independence came in a lot of packages. That same summer of 1978 was a big one for Hal, who recalled, "When I was eight, I got to fly to South Africa alone to spend a month with our grandparents. I had fun visiting and meeting cousins and even my great-grandmother."

Hal said, "A call to any of our grandparents [maternal in the UK and paternal in South Africa] happened only a couple of times a year because it was extremely expensive and we had maybe two minutes to talk. So when we had the chance, we were pretty excited to talk, albeit quickly. I did exchange written letters with them."

Because the exchange rate between South Africa and the U.S. was not in favor of the Brigish grandparents, and because learning the skills of travel would be useful their whole lives, it made sense to send the children to visit them. In 1980, when Jackie was six, she and Hal flew together to spend a month in South Africa at grandparents Harry and Fanny's flat in Johannesburg. Hal recalled,

"We went to game parks to see the animals, drove to the beach in Durban. My grandfather bought me a cricket kit and taught me the basics of how to play in the park across the street."

Equal Responsibilities

Susan Grunthal expressed strong admiration for the way that Joyce and Alan parented. "I think Joyce and Alan gave all the cues. And in my opinion, they're unusual parents from the point of view of not only how they treated Cy, but how they passed on that message to their children, and their friends."

For instance, Cy always had chores. And because he was being included in everything, he was included in responsibility as well as privilege. And that really seems to have made a huge difference in the way that he works in the world. Cy and Hal are six and four years older, respectively, than Jackie. The boys had been helping with household tasks for a while when Jackie joined the chore corps.

Sister Jackie recalled, "Chores were a part of life. We liked them as much as my kids like them now. I think it's notable that the chores Cy had were the same as ours. As much as possible Mom tried *not* to treat us differently. We all had to make our beds and keep our rooms clean. Other than chores for extra pay like mowing the lawn, the household chores were the same for all three of us—setting the table, cleaning, garbage, washing dishes—consequences, too.

"We were definitely not angelic children! None of us. Consequences were loss of privileges like watching TV or bedtimes. We had set chores that rotated weekly, so if Cy was setting the table, I may have been clearing the table, and Hal helped with dishes or garbage or something like that. But things got done, and we were held responsible—all three of us."

Joyce was quick to cite Staples School in Westport, where Cy attended the inclusion program, whose curriculum offered a lot of that kind of experience. They had a little house and the children had to "run" the little house like a big house, learning all sorts of skills. As a group, the children were taught to prepare their lunch. "So I wouldn't say it was all me," said Joyce, "but certainly continuity was us, because a lot of his friends don't participate in those kinds of life maintenance activities."

Joyce constantly encouraged other parents to teach their children with disabilities to do chores and take part in the upkeep of the household, something that would affirm that they were needed, and that they could learn to take pride in the tasks. That encouragement resulted in a continuum of responses. As usual, it takes time and patience to teach life skills which will promote responsibility and foster independence.

Joyce always had the far-seeing eye, and she knew that later, when the children and parents had aged somewhat, the elders would be grateful, whether or not the children were living independently, to have their children be skilled at helping out. Joyce always held that those were things that they could and should achieve, and that learning those responsibilities would help the young ones to understand that they had an integral place in the working of the family.

Nurturing Cy's Independence

When fostering independence in a growing child, one walks the fine line of privilege and responsibility. Would that the world and its inhabitants had only rounded corners and no sharp edges. The best of guides help us to provide young adventurers with trust and caution, and solid instruction—and with luck, a strong safety net. Not so for many. Joyce taught Cy well, and gave him rein, but he'd been such an adventurous and rascally little musketeer, it must have given Alan and Joyce pause now and again as Cy learned to navigate the greater world.

Chapter 24

CLASP—COMMUNITY LEAGUE ADVOCATES FOR SPECIAL PEOPLE

Along the way, Joyce and Alan had met and enjoyed friendships with other families who had also chosen to raise their children with disabilities at home. Joyce became interested in CLASP (Community League Advocate for Special People), a small organization which had been in existence for a number of years in the area.[32] She and Alan got involved in the group homes aspect, which led them to participate in the recreation aspect as parents were expected to participate in the organization.

CLASP sponsored a lot of sports activities for several reasons—helping to keep the children healthy and fit, not the least of them. But there was more. In our American culture, being highly competitive is revered. But the population of special people so long isolated from that culture does not necessarily share the same values. Inclusion transcends winning.

Special Olympics

In the very early 1980s, Coleytown (CDC) turned over the sponsorship of the Special Olympics team to CLASP, whose members were from all around the area. In a news article many years later, Joyce explained, "We work at developing the handicapped kids' interest in sports. They have fun

---

32 Currently known as "Our Vision," and headed up by Julie McNamee, who had been involved when Joyce was running CLASP.

participating even though some may not care about heavy-duty competition."[33]

Two years later, Rob Nathan, CLASP member and Special Olympics athlete Timmy Harmon's coach, spoke candidly about the value of the experience. About Timmy, Coach Nathan said, 'He gets such pleasure just from being able to compete. He doesn't care if he wins or loses; it's sort of pure athleticism . . . If you give these kids a goal, some high expectation, they really will rise to it."[34]

Again, the same sentiment is expressed by a member of the volleyball team, exemplifying the crux of the matter for people with disabilities. About the 1995 Special Olympics World Games held at Yale Bowl (the largest sporting event in the world that year, hosting 7,000 athletes from 140 countries), a member of the silver medal volleyball team said, "We had a blast. We tried to do our best. And I hope I get a chance to do this again."[35]

Not a word about winning, but rather about the joy, the attempt, and the opportunity.

Coaching

Geri Price had founded CLASP, and Alan and Joyce admired Geri's leadership. When Geri moved away, Joyce stepped in as administrator. Joyce trained and got certified to coach track and field. Several friends helped with coaching runners and those who enjoyed shot put and discus.

Joyce also coached the CLASP swim team for Special Olympics for a number of years—usually with twelve to fifteen swimmers, with a broad range of disabilities. They trained at the pool at the Y, where there was a lifeguard. She said it was easy to run the lessons from the edge of the pool. She had no formal assistants, but parents were there and would jump in if any of the kids had a problem in the pool.

Because Joyce's expectations for behavior and learning have always been high, and because Cy's way in the world has resulted from those consistent practices, she was always grateful for parents who appreciated and carried out that consistency, and was deeply frustrated by those parents who did not share those expectations, who weren't encouraging responsibility or who were not consistent with the kids. It remained an issue for her that she could not resolve.

---

33 O'Neil, Liz. "Weston's Joyce Brigish—a Very Special Person." *Westport News* on June 23, 1989.

34 Jagerson. Ty. *Westport News*, "Swimming is special to Timmy." March 27, 1991.

35 D'Amico, Marianne. "Games End in Glee." *The Hour*, July 10, 1995.

Joyce was courageous escorting so many children at a time with her chaperones to new experiences and venues, and she did it all through the joy of recreation. She was adept at setting parameters and was firm in holding the children to them. Coming along, having a guide is necessary—to show the way, warn about pitfalls, discuss and model appropriate behavior for safety and enjoyment. Being taught the ropes is receiving a gift. Joyce didn't play when it came to honoring commitments. Through that stern practice, she allowed the children to try on new behaviors and adhere to rules, which gave them the opportunity to be proud of new achievements while having fun.

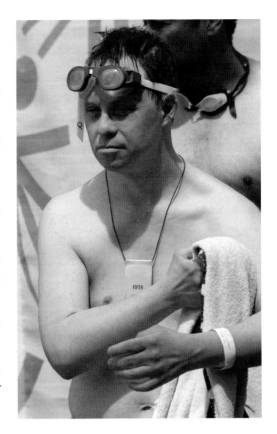

Pool Etiquette

But what happened before getting into the pool and after getting out required coaching as well. Sequential actions that might be taken for granted with a "normal" population needed careful attention with the children with disabilities. Joyce helped them locate their lockers, and then gave them three-part instructions for getting ready to swim: "1. get undressed in front of your own locker, 2. immediately, put on your swimsuit, and then 3. head to the pool."

The swimmers also learned from sequential instructions their after-swim protocol. "1. you return from the pool, 2. you dry yourself off, 3. you take your swimsuit off; 4. you quickly put on your underwear, so that you look respectable." Joyce made sure that public pool etiquette was adhered to, to make clear to the children who had not as yet had locker room experience that they were not to wander around with nothing on. For some, this was really new behavior.

Jackie Becomes a Volunteer

It didn't take long, of course, for CLASP and Special Olympics to become a full-family affair. Jackie joined CLASP as a volunteer when she was ten. As Jackie says, "I was always a mature child. I was given more responsibilities

than most kids my age." She helped out with indoor recreation with 20–30 children with special needs on Saturday mornings. Jackie described playing games, supervising such things as relay races in the swimming pool and basketball skirmishes, as "very enjoyable."

Even at that age, Jackie wanted to be a teacher, so she was somewhat of a natural. "There was so much unconditional love and attention. I just had fun working with the kids, helping them, playing games, facilitating things and helping to organize. I enjoyed that."

Not every Special Olympics group had individual "buddies," but CLASP had instituted the "one-to-one" companion to each individual athlete. That meant being in charge of the schedule and helping the athlete get up, dressed, and ready for a day of events (while everyone else was getting ready as well), accompanying the athlete to the Olympic activities and taking them to "Olympic Town."

Every athlete wore a lanyard that contained pertinent information: their names, and scheduled events and times. The one-on-ones made sure that the athletes arrived on time and were ready to participate in each event. During time off, they accompanied the athletes to Olympic Town to eat and enjoy other activities, or watch their friends participate in other events. Jackie said, "I would always be given somebody who I could manage based on my age. Because, again, I was among the youngest doing that, at least when I started."

Other students occasionally joined in to help out. But Jackie continued volunteering until she graduated from high school. She was honored by CLASP for volunteering for five years for CLASP and seven for the Special Olympics.

Chapter 25

1981

JOYCE AS ADVOCATE

S usan Grunthal noted that "a very important aspect of Joyce's relationship to children with disabilities is her dedication to supporting—and
diligence in expanding—organizations that serve them."

Joyce spoke about recognizing intelligence and recognizing bad habits
(habitual, inappropriate, or poor behavior) that require constant attention in
order to replace them with behavior more appropriate. Her role was to be an
unflagging gentle but firm (sometimes very firm) reminder. She was adamant that the children could indeed learn to change habits, but that "there's
only success if you get the participation of the parents." The continuity of
those expectations and monitoring of the behavioral changes for progress
and support must happen at home as well as during whatever classroom or
programming the children are involved in. Without constancy, the changes
rarely hold. Parents must be active participants in the process of change and
helping their children to meet expectations.

She knew it would be necessary to push traditional teaching ap-
proaches to the wayside and think creatively about the ways and means
of educating people with disabilities as well as enlightening those without. In order to further illuminate her understanding of how to bridge
understanding, Joyce attended Fairfield University to study advocacy for
people with disabilities.

In a news article, Hannah Elsas Miller[36] describes a new program, "Understanding Handicaps," originated at the Meeting Street School in Rhode
Island, which was "specifically designed to prepare students to deal with

---

36 Author of *Films in the Classroom—A Practical Guide.* Scarecrow Press. 1979.

those less able to function and manage daily activities in a normal setting." Joyce attended one of those workshops in Rhode Island.

Kate Dickstein was the coordinator of the program in Westport. Sessions were held for adults and children, and by role-playing participants learned to experience a variety of disabilities.

Most were grateful for the information as it helped to make them more comfortable around people with handicaps. Ms. Miller, who "changed her career [as a physical education teacher] when she became slightly disabled" and required a wheelchair, was a "participating member of the workshop held for teachers and administrators" and eventually became a guest speaker in the program. About the groups of middle school students she visited through the program, she wrote, "Their attentiveness, sensitivity and pointed questions show their interest and fascination with the subject of handicaps . . . Most students are open and honest in their reaction and as a result their many questions about handicaps are answered during the program and a lot of humanization takes place."

Joyce became a workshop leader for the program. In Westport, she was asked to teach the program across all the grades. She also held sessions for teachers. What she wanted most was to cultivate compassion, and to diminish fear and discomfort and the embarrassment of not knowing how to interact with people with disabilities. That would lead, she hoped, to easier communication and better understanding, and "Understanding Handicaps" had that potential.

Joyce said, "I was an advocate there for the special needs families, as well as for the schools. I worked for either the families who had issues with the schools, or with the schools who had issues with families—but never the two at the same time. Some parents saw what I'd done with Cy and the reading skills and math skills, and they asked if I could work with their kids. And so I would just spend hours with them."

About his mother's work in the schools, Hal said, "I think it opened up a lot of people's eyes." Joyce would have the students put socks on their hands and then try to button and write and pick things up. She had discussions with the students about vision and hearing disabilities. She used blindfolds and ear muffs to simulate vision and hearing loss, orthotics and a wheelchair, and led role-playing exercises. As the activities were interactive, they were highly successful in their ability to raise awareness and compassion, and there was room for discussion following the exercises.

"But," Joyce said, "mainly we had speakers who talked about each of the areas of [their own] disabilities." For instance, a man who used a wheelchair did a presentation and spoke about the difficulty of maneuvering in public. At that time "wheelchair accessible" was not yet a known term. There were no ramps at street corners and few at the entrances to businesses.

Joyce continued, "And in fact one time Cy was a speaker. I thought, *Well, I'm sure I can coach him to do this. To talk about what it's like to be 'mentally retarded.'* I brought him in. And he talked a bit and then the main thing was for them to ask him questions because a lot of kids—and adults—are too scared to ask questions. They just back off. And so here was an opportunity to ask questions and to realize that you're not going to be judged for what you ask. And the questions were generally good, and he answered them well."

Hal recalled that the disabilities of the school kids ranged from drastic—barely able to communicate—to slight. Some of Cy's friends were able to learn to drive and got their licenses. Joyce was quick to add, "But that doesn't mean to say they should have."

Understanding the variety of disabilities was a challenge, as was communicating that a person who required a wheelchair because of a physical disability—but who had no cognitive disability—was different from someone who needs to be fed and bathed.

Ms. Miller wrote, "Being fed makes one realize what it feels like not to be able to regulate the amount of food and the speed at which one has to chew and swallow. Trying to communicate without words simulates the loss of hearing just as watching a film without the soundtrack. Anger, fear, and frustration are expressed by all who participate, and much understanding is the result of the simulations."

About the "Understanding Handicaps" program, Hannah Elsas Miller wrote, "Although there has been no scientific evaluation, the students' written and oral response has been positive proof of the results of the program. As expected, if children and adults have more information, confusion and fear will give way to understanding."[37]

Advocacy and Baseball

After Joyce had run a week-long program at the Weston Middle School as part of the ongoing effort to familiarize students with their fellow students who had disabilities, her charges wanted to do something as a group with the children who were "handicapped." Alan's best friend, Bill Bertin, encouraged Joyce to set up a baseball game and helped her organize it.[38] Mark

---

37 Miller, Hannah Elsas. "Understanding the Handicapped." (no newspaper name, n.d.) Westport. From the family scrapbook.

38 Lenci, Susan Haas. "Weston Kids Play Ball; Some Are Handicapped." No newspaper title. [June] 1981.

Bertin recalled that he and his dad enjoyed the game so much that Bill wanted to share it with everybody.

Many hands helped make the June 11 game a success. Bill Bertin served as umpire. Weston Parks and Recreation loaned the CLASP "team" real baseball

uniforms and the Little League in town came to help out, creating a buddy system so two played each position. When a CLASP student was at bat, a Little Leaguer ran the bases with him or her. Ordinarily these CLASP students were spectators at their brothers' and sisters' games. In this game, though, they got to participate. This game made dreams come true.

Bill is described as "kind, gentle, and enthusiastic." When he died suddenly in September of 1982, his family created the Bill Bertin Memorial Fund, which provided annual support for the continuation of the baseball game between students in Weston and members of CLASP. In June of 1983 Alan opened the first Bill Bertin Memorial Baseball Game in honor of Bill's participation and love of the sport. Bill's wife, Phyllis (who advised Joyce on teaching Cy to read), provided a baseball shirt for each participant as well. The game was played annually for more than a dozen years. In a June 1990 *Westport News* story, Joyce said, "Virtually every special child plays in this game. Blind, physically or mentally handicapped, deaf—it makes no difference to us."[39]

Impacting Lives

Joyce's advocacy work and the resulting desire by the middle school students to get involved is a fine example of education not being a one-way street. Working or playing together, we are all affected to some degree. Those with

---

39 *Westport News*, Friday, June 15, 1990. "Baseball is Special to these Special Youngsters."

disabilities, including those whose disabilities may not be so apparent, and those without learn in many ways—about our comfort levels, our willingness to burst the barriers of our own shyness or possibly undiscovered prejudices—and what Joyce always hoped: that we would discover the common ground of our creativity and resourcefulness and find success together.

Many have been very fond of Cy. Old friends of Hal's told him that when they got together with other mutual friends from childhood, Cy came up in their conversation about how much he had impacted their lives.

Mark Bertin, Bill and Phyllis's son, was active in the community of people with disabilities.

Starting around age twelve, Mark began volunteering for Special Olympics, which he continued to do for a long time. "Special Olympics and my time with the Brigishes were all related in some ways. I spent a lot of time working one-on-one with the athletes, going away with them for weekends. Those years were a time for self-discovery."

Mark continued the same type of volunteering through college. His plan was to be a general physician, specializing in developmental pediatrics, and then that field became his complete focus.[40] Mark wrote:

> "Whenever I'm asked how I ended up in the field of developmental pediatrics, I start with my neighbors growing up, the Brigishes. Our families were (and are) entwined in friendship, with Cy a regular happy presence at their pool and in all the activities we attended together. Joyce set a high standard for Cy, advocating for his needs while also firmly and lovingly pushing him to achieve more. Involvement with Joyce's Special Olympic group was a life-changing, life-saving part of my world during a time of intense personal struggle.
>
> "Joyce's mentorship of the program was a role model of honesty, strength and compassionate guidance benefiting Cy and the other children, as well as all the volunteers and staff. Among all the children of the Special Olympics group, Cy was never-endingly upbeat, polite, fun, sweet natured and well-mannered. Much of that followed from his mother's guiding presence, through all the challenges of childhood. Never allowing Cy's disability to hinder excessively his education, activities, or family time, Joyce urged him forward into becoming the largely independent and always kind adult he has become.

---

40 Dr. Bertin is now a practicing developmental pediatrician who's written three books about child development. His most recent, *How Children Thrive*, released in May 2018, has been lauded as "an elegant, effective, yet simple approach." For information about him and his work, see https://www.developmentaldoctor.com/.

"Long before the field of developmental disabilities had caught up and caught on, Joyce was advocating for everything children with disabilities require to thrive as adults. Potential is not linked only to a standardized, by definition limited, measure of abilities. Children reach their potential when well educated, and encouraged to be independent; engaged and part of the community; receiving supports at both a family and a community level; and accepted by the people around them. Being an advocate for a child is everything in making sure all of these supports are ongoing and in place, barriers are removed when possible, and long terms goals and planning are sustained. Long before that became, as they say in the field, 'standard of care,' Joyce had it all figured out."

Chapter 26

VOLUNTEER COACHES

Joyce had wanted to take the volunteers from her area to the annual Connecticut Special Olympics. "If I didn't know them really well, I would work with them a week before Special Olympics to tell them what I expected of them; that this is not *their* fun. This is the fun of the athletes, but I hoped they'd get a lot out of it."

Hal had started running because Alan was a runner, and that translated into Hal helping out at the training for the Special Olympics as well. He also worked with Cy with his straight-line sprints to prepare him to run the dashes, standing at the end of the distance and calling to Cy so he'd run all the way to the end in a straight line and not get disqualified. Due to Joyce's advocacy work in the schools, quite a few students from Hal's school also volunteered.

Both Hal and Jackie noted that Joyce found good coaches, and high school athletes and friends of Hal, Jackie, and Cy would join in to help out. Jackie recalled, "Many of the same volunteers returned year after year to Special Olympics because Mom made it fun for the volunteers, too, bringing wine, cheese, beer for the adults in the evenings."

Hal recalled that as a teenage coach, he would help the runners by showing them how to run—"follow me, do what I do," teaching them what he was learning from his own running coaches. "In track, there're not a lot of rules. You go from Point A to Point B and then there's certain things you can do to make yourself go faster. When we first started going to Special Olympics, it was really more about participation. There weren't a whole lot of rules, but as the years went along they started getting stricter."

So they worked on staying in the lane for track *and* for swimming. Someone would stand at the end of the lane calling Cy's name to keep him

from touching the lane dividers, which would have gotten him disqualified. Another friend of Cy's was a natural swimmer, but his social nature outstripped his desire to compete. He could swim really fast, but he so enjoyed waving to the people in the stands that it was difficult to keep him on task. Another of Cy's swimming buddies was a powerhouse at freestyle, but he was so focused, he'd forget to breathe.

In the true essence of the natural teacher, Hal said, "You kind of just have to look at everyone individually to figure out what they need—to figure out what events each of the athletes was best suited for."

Chapter 27

A NEW FAMILY MEMBER

Most of the family had always wanted a dog, but even though Joyce and Alan both had dogs when they were young, Alan really didn't want one. Nonetheless in a conversation in December of 1982, "in a weak moment," he let it be known that if they were ever to have a dog it should be a golden retriever. Though his birthday is in May, a puppy named Simba arrived in January wearing a ribbon and a tag that said "Happy Birthday!" The whole family fell in love with that puppy and so began "the Brigish–golden retriever mutual admiration society," evidenced by the succession of beloved canines that followed: Fabian, Nadia, Shayna, Rugby, Zach, and Jeter.

That pup grew into a lovely dog that Alan refers to as "Simba, the Magnificent." Of course, though Basil was long gone, Joyce had had a succession of birds to add to the already lively household. The only thing simple in this family's complex lives was that all birds were named Basil (I, II, III, and IV).

Joyce was juggling any number of things—as always—and heaven forbid there should be no drama. One day while the roof was being repaired, the current bird, Basil III, flew out through the sliding glass doors and up to the roof. Joyce called to the worker on the roof asking, "Please catch him." The bird was retrieved and brought back in. The bird got out again. This prompts the question: Was Joyce or the bird more determined? He flew high up into a very tall tree.

Joyce called Hal to come and help get the bird. She also called Simba to help out. Hal and Joyce climbed the tree and reached the bird. Hal somehow inspired the bird to fly down to the ground. Joyce yelled to Simba to hold the bird. And the dog put his nose on the bird's body, pinning it until Joyce and Hal descended and could return the bird to the indoors. Formidable.

Hal in Middle School (Cy is 16), C. 1984

When Hal and Cy were in their mid-teens, their interests broadened and opportunities for maturing presented themselves.

Because of Joyce's work and because of Cy, all the Brigishes had a reputation for openness and inclusion. When a new student enrolled at Hal's middle school, it's not surprising that Hal was asked to help him negotiate his new surroundings. Erik Weihenmayer[41] had diminishing vision and Hal was the perfect buddy.

"I was assigned to take him around early on," said Hal. "We became really good friends for a long time. He and I used to hang out quite a bit and we would go riding bicycles, and he was always down for any adventure, even if he couldn't see. He would follow me on his own bicycle and he would just listen. We'd go to Devil's Den and all sorts of stuff."[42]

"Down for any adventure" is surely the definitive phrase. Later on, Erik would trek the entire 277 miles of the Grand Canyon and climb the tallest mountain on every continent, achieving fame as the first blind man to climb Mount Everest. It's easy to understand why today he is a motivational speaker.

Truly, one might wonder how that is possible. In 2018, he appeared on *The View*, to surprise his onetime fifth-grade English student, *View* co-host Meghan McCain. His foundation, No Barriers, as he said on the show, has helped 5,000 people break through their barriers and also instituted a veterans program. He described the work of the foundation as being "about growing that light inside and using that as fuel and vision to power you through a lot of challenges."[43]

---

41 More about Erik at his website: http://www.touchthetop.com/about-erik.

42 Devil's Den is the local nature preserve.

43 https://abcnews.go.com/Entertainment/meghan-mccain-surprised-5th-grade-teacher-teacher-appreciation/story?id=55013628—a wonderful clip from *The View* where Erik Weihemayer made a surprise visit to his former student Meghan McCain on teacher appreciation day.

Chapter 28

AS IF THERE WASN'T ENOUGH GOING ON

The family remained involved throughout the year in sports activities. Cy had also always loved music. He had a record player and a small collection of music that he really liked and would play repeatedly. He and Hal would listen to Billy Joel and Michael Jackson and the Village People, all of whom were Cy's favorites. Cy knew all the words and enjoyed singing on his microphone. Proving the boy was born to "tread the boards," he'd perform for Hal or for himself. Hal recalled that the cabana by the pool was a perfect place to put on a show. The word "ham" has been applied to Cy more than once. Joyce gave up sculpting in 1984, and she and her friend Joan Starr opened a gallery, Images Sculptural Concepts in Norwalk. They showcased more than fifty contemporary sculptors whose work spanned from the realistic to the abstract. But even though she had a job that could be consuming, Joyce's work with young people did not diminish.

CLASP Trips

Two things that were important to Joyce were respite for parents and, for the children, getting an introduction into the real world beyond their local community. She was troubled that they had so few experiences and memories about which they could say "I'm proud of that."

She organized a group of forty school-age children with the idea of expanding their horizons beyond the community. The children had never visited a museum, had never been on a cruise ship (Joyce hadn't either), hadn't been on vacations.

With three adults and one college student as chaperones, she took them to Washington, D.C., on their first trip. As they visited museums, she explained to them what the museums were all about—and they enjoyed it. They visited Air and Space and the Hirschhorn at the Smithsonian. Joyce said, "In particular, they had a most wonderful time at the National Geographic museum. They still remind me when I see them." That first trip to the nation's capital began a tradition of travel for the group.

Joyce was always "very fussy about what they ate." So, before they went on a trip together, whether a cruise or Disney World, she cautioned them to be sensible about their meals. She had a rule about buffets. Holding up three fingers, she'd say, "You've got to walk around three times—three—one, two, three—with no plate in your hand, and see what's available." She knew that otherwise they would heap their plates. If someone hadn't stuck to the plan and piled up a plate anyway, she or one of the chaperones would ask for the heaped plate and remove half of what was on it so that they wouldn't get sick from overeating.

The adults included teachers and relatives of the students, and the trips allowed them to experience what the group was experiencing, some learning the ropes of chaperoning long-distance trips and others visiting a museum or a destination for the first time.

Most things went smoothly, but now and again Joyce would have to have a serious discussion with one of the children for violating the trust of the group by misbehaving. She understood that some of them were not used to parameters being drawn and upheld, but she was adamant that the children learn to take responsibility for their actions and to deserve the trust of their peers and chaperones. In delivering a reprimand, Joyce was conversational but firm, and let the offender know that she believed he or she was capable of living up to the agreement of good behavior.

Traveling as a Way to Teach Life Skills:
Eating, Packing, Dressing

A number of parents had to be enlightened not just about how to teach life skills; they didn't know that their children could learn new behaviors, and break bad habits. The teaching is the same as with any child *without* developmental delays. It just requires more repetition to create new behaviors and therefore an investment of more time. But it most certainly can be done.

Before the first trip, Joyce invited the parents of the CLASP members to her house to share her expectations. "Look, I'm taking them on a trip. You all admire Cy because of his manners and his behavior, etc. I want all the kids to be like Cy. And hopefully it will stick with them when they come home. And then you will appreciate what it is to live with a Cy.

"Some parents didn't listen to me, and some of them really worked on their kids. I said, 'When they get changed, they get changed in private. I don't want to see your son or daughter walking in the nude; that's not going to happen on my watch.' I shouldn't have to tell the parent, you know, 'We've got to watch what your child does and how they do it.' And they paid attention to how they eat in the restaurant—some of them paid attention. But they didn't pay attention to the fact that I wanted their kids to be able to pack the suitcase up at the end of the trip.

"I was very strict with Cy, as I was with the others. It was important to me that his behavior was appropriate for the rest of the world to see. And I had instructed the parents: I need your children to know how to eat appropriately in the restaurants and how to behave appropriately in front of the public. It's very important, because I'll send them home as quickly as they got here. And some of the parents you could see worked on their kids. Because when I walked around the restaurant, and I saw one fellow sitting there with his roll on the plate, and his knife and fork, and the butter there, cutting up his bread, I knew that the parents had worked with him. But one girl could barely carry her suitcase. No one had overseen her packing, and she brought all of her exercise weights. She had more weights than clothes."

Aside from travel, the group was training weekly for the games. The Connecticut Special Olympics began to host Fall Games in 1984 and grew exponentially. Within five years they would include "more than 500 coaches and volunteers" and ran for two days.[44]

---

44 *Westport News*, "Locals Competing in Fall Special Olympics," Friday, December 1, 1989. No author.

Chapter 29

THE WORDS
NO PARENT WANTS
TO HEAR

Cy would continue to have many medical issues. He's always hated Band-Aids, and still will not allow one to be applied. But his parents' biggest battle was to get him to understand that he would have to have injections, sometimes be admitted to the hospital, perhaps have more surgery. Joyce offered continual assurance. "I will always be with you in the hospital, and I will be with you until you go to sleep for surgery, and I'll be with you when you wake up. Or we will be with you. And we always stuck to it. We never let him down."

The family has had more than its share of opportunities to hold to that promise. During a routine physical for Special Olympics, Cy's pediatrician made a discovery that turned out to be cancer.

Joyce recalled the evening when she shared the news about Cy's diagnosis with Alan. "We were very emotional." However, in an attempt to console his parents, Cy approached them, arms outstretched, and with exceptional wisdom said, "Hug each other. Love each other, and everything will turn out fine."[45]

Surgery was successful, but it was followed by a long period of radiation. Unfortunately, the site was over-radiated and the muscles in Cy's

---

45 Hurley, Johanna. "Local Man Overcomes Many Obstacles." *The Weston Voice*, February 13, 1992.

leg atrophied as they lost strength, resulting in his leg not being able to hold his weight.

"We took him to his oncologist at Yale who had become a friend of ours and of Cy's. And she wrote a paper on the subject." The follow-up was that Cy had to have physical therapy done almost daily. Joyce continued to work with him daily on his speech as well. She provided constant encouragement and really pushed his swimming. Joyce and Alan kept a close eye on him, because he could easily have developed another form of cancer as a result of the type he had had. They were most grateful that he did not. It took some time, but Cy recovered his strength and balance—and his dancing feet!

Chapter 30

THE SOCIAL GRACES

Though the family lived in Weston, Cy went to high school in the neighboring town of Westport because they had a special education inclusion program. Cy had a girlfriend, Gracie. The two loved to dance and cut a rug together at the high school prom, which was held at the Westin Hotel in Stamford. Proud Granny Dora was visiting for one such event.

When Hal's band was playing at the middle school, he asked his parents if Cy could come to the dance with Gracie. It was fine with Alan and Joyce and they suggested Hal ask Cy. Well, Cy loved the idea and asked Gracie to come along. When her father, Joe, brought her to the house, Cy asked to speak to him privately. They went to the front lawn of the house and Cy asked Joe for permission to marry Gracie.

Joe was flabbergasted. But Cy said he understood they'd have to wait, but that he wanted Joe's permission. Joe agreed they'd have to wait until after graduation, and that was fine with Cy.

Alan and Joyce decided to go to the dance, "Because," as Joyce said, "these kids at the school don't know Cy and Gracie, and kids can be brutal." The four rode together and Alan parked, though he didn't realize he was in a handicapped parking spot, not having seen the small sign. The policeman (who knew everybody—it was a small community) tapped on Alan's window and asked him to move as it was a handicapped zone. Rarely the wallflower, Cy opened his window and said, "Excuse me. Can't you see that I'm handicapped? I have Down syndrome." Joyce said, "The policeman looked at him and turned ashen." He apologized and allowed them to remain. Alan said, "No. He can walk. Yes, he's handicapped, but he can walk. That was my error. We'll move."

On to the party! Both Cy and Gracie like to dance fast and to breakdance. Gracie does her own thing. She usually copies him, or he will sometimes copy her.

Another of Cy's friends was there, but not dancing. She mostly stood by the food table drinking soda and eating snacks. Joyce saw her go to the phones and make a call, then she disappeared outside. Joyce was concerned about her, so she went outside and saw the girl get picked up by a member of her family.

The next day Joyce asked the girl's mother what she'd told her about the dance. Her mom said that she'd danced with everybody and had the most wonderful time.

Joyce felt she had to tell the mother that it wasn't true and that the girl hadn't danced, but probably wanted her mom to think that she was just like all the other kids. Joyce said, "Cy was upset that she hadn't come with anybody to dance with, and have a good time. He was very sensitive to that. Hal said to us afterwards the kids in his grade who were there just loved Cy and Gracie. They thought they were wonderful. But they didn't get a chance to love [the other girl]. And that upset me terribly because she deserved that just as much." This speaks volumes about Joyce's depth of compassion and an underlying reason for her dedication to inclusion.

Cy had had ample opportunity to practice life skills, and one of those is quiet observation. "Even today," Joyce said, "I talk to him about certain things that some of his friends do that are not appropriate and they don't look good. Like stubbornness—Cy's stubborn, but not as stubborn as some. Cy recognizes people [with Down syndrome] by some of the things they do. He'll say to me, 'Did you see that boy over there? He's a Downie.' And I'll say, 'Okay. What can you tell me about him?' He'll say, 'He's probably stubborn, like I was.' He does know what's going on."

Family friend Judy Machanik was thoughtful about his observations. "I think Cy has the ability to absorb what's going on around him in a way that's way past what we can really understand. I've watched him in social settings,

and he can almost wrap himself in the code of good behavior in a situation." At a wedding both families attended, he was "watching people and seeing how they move about. He's very observant and, I think, inhales what's going on around him, and is able to discern what feels right and what feels wrong . . . So I think that there's a lot going on that we don't know. . . you read that on his face, and [in] his body language."

Westport News contributor Sean Flavin wrote, "Cy is great because while he is often horsing around, he can also be serious. I can talk to Cy about

many more involved matters, because he is very intelligent and has a special understanding of people and events."[46]

Alan says, "This is still true. He'll sit in on a conversation, not say a word, and then quote verbatim from what was said, with full understanding."

Judy continued, "Sometimes I've watched him sort of sink back into a couch, if he's feeling not so comfortable with what's going on."

On the other hand, when Cy has

---

46 Flavin, Sean D. "Connecticut Special Olympics Spotlight Special People." *Westport News,* July 6, 1988.

something to say to a group, he doesn't hesitate to address them. Joyce said, "When he's somewhere where people are talking, he needs to talk, too. And he must think very quickly about what he's going to say, because he never thinks ahead."

Judy said, "He makes it very clear that he wants to speak. And then he expects everybody to listen." A case in point was at Alan's surprise seventieth birthday party in 2012 when Cy spontaneously stepped to the mic to wish Alan a happy birthday and to tell the crowd how much he loved his dad.

A certain cognitive level is required in order to be able to speak well on the spur of the moment, to be engaging, funny, or both; and a sense of self is necessary. Cy has all that—part innate showman, and part having had the encouragement and the occasions to join in, say what's on his mind, and be honored for his contribution.

Cy can be very funny, but he's also pensive, an observer. He's been given ample opportunity to observe others, which taps into his natural curiosity, and his tendency is to describe what he discerns. He feels deeply and is quite candid.

Judy said that "Cy's been raised to

understand that he's feeling all kinds of things, and that's really fine, and when it's appropriate [he] can express those feelings in a social setting." At a dinner gathering, Cy sensed that two of the guests were having some marital issues. "He got up and he addressed them, in a very touching and supportive and loving way. Essentially what he said was I know that these two people are having a problem, and that makes me really sad. And I hope that they'll be able to fix it."

People quickly took up other conversations. "That was, I think," Judy continued, "an example of encouraging him to know what he was feeling, to be able to articulate what he was feeling—and to do it. To have watched Cy evolve into the kind of person that he is has been a real gift."

Chapter 31

HAL LEAVES FOR COLLEGE

1987

While Hal and his friends were in high school, they took Cy to all kinds of gatherings and events. But once Hal was studying at Syracuse and his buddies had also gone off to college, Cy was understandably left behind. And their absence in his life was palpable.

As usual, Joyce had an idea about how to rectify that situation. She wrote a letter to the newspaper putting out a call specifically to the young people of Weston for companionship for Cy and other young adults with special needs. She suggested a schedule of once every five weeks to offer friendship, stating that what other young people take for granted is often out of reach for young people with disabilities, who just want to have the same experiences as any other teenager.

Initial efforts to engage peers had gleaned no volunteers. Joyce's campaign for providing peer companionship was picked up by the Weston High School's newspaper.[47] Sean Flavin wrote a lovely article offering a description of what a buddy does, and it may have turned the tide. Flavin explained, "A buddy is someone who is willing to spend a little time with any of the twenty-six handicapped children in the area, doing such activities as going for pizza, seeing a movie, or going to a high school basketball game. It's not a hard job, but to the handicapped children, it can make a world of difference."

Six months later, Flavin, who also had a sibling in CLASP, wrote briefly and poignantly about the division between populations. "It's really kind

---

47 Flavin, Sean D. "Share a Little Love." *The Weston Beat,* February 17, 1988.

of ridiculous the way lines are drawn between 'us' and 'them.' Where the disabilities leave a void, love and laughter comes in to fill it. And being a part of that love and laughter is a process I will never forget."[48] Jackie recalled that Sean became Cy's primary buddy for several years and they spent much time together outside of Special Olympics. He'd take Cy out to the movies or just hang out together. Jackie's boyfriend, Dan Parker, was also his buddy just for Special Olympics, as Cy always requested him.

Horizons and athletic opportunities were expanding. In 1988, the CLASP athletes headed to Disney World for a week.[49] The twenty-six athletes were accompanied by sixteen chaperones, including Jackie. The group worked diligently to raise money; private individuals and companies contributed as well.[50]

While Joyce's advocacy for people with disabilities was in full swing, Alan had been running his business, Information Systems Marketing (ISM), a communications and electronic information services consulting firm, from 1979 to 1983. His uncanny sense of business trends, in particular how online technology was evolving, made him a much-sought-after consultant and speaker in the very earliest days of online information distribution and marketing—and kept him very busy.

Taking what he'd learned from those days, he assembled an experienced team of former colleagues and founded Videolog Communications, an online catalog of electronic components, with electronic design engineers as its target audience. They raised venture and institutional money and launched the business in 1983, achieving a certain amount of support from the industry, though the company was way ahead of its time. Many of the elements instituted at Videolog are common today in online advertising and selling. They shuttered the business in 1988.

The Information Industry Association's Electronic Services Division awarded Alan its 1988 Entrepreneur Award.[51]

---

48 Flavin. Sean D. "Connecticut Special Olympics Spotlight Special People." *Westport News*, July 6, 1988.

49 *Westport News*, "Next Stop: Disney World," Friday, September 18, 1988.

50 Purnell, Alexandra S. "26 Children Pack Bags for Disney World Visit," The Hour, (n.d.)

51 "Brigish Receives Award," newspaper clipping, (n.d., no banner)

Chapter 32

1989

CY GRADUATES

W hen Hal finished his sopho-
more year, Cy graduated from
two high schools: Weston
High School(fiscally responsible for Cy's out-
of-town tuition) and Staples High School in
Westport (where he attended the inclusion
program), as he was enrolled in both—and
because Joyce insisted. Ever the jokesters, the
family presented Cy with the news of the day.

Joyce continued to run CLASP, helping
to keep the young folks fit for the annual
Special Olympics. In December, they

participated in the two-day Connecticut Special Olympics Fifth Annual Fall Games, which had begun in 1984. Bowling would be a popular but separate event.[52]

Increasing involvement from organizations in the surrounding towns that donated funds for Special Olympics and provided a multitude of venues for the events testified to her success in blending the larger community with the community of people with disabilities.

It's daunting to think of all the organization time and skill it must have taken to keep not only the athletic training going, but all the other activities—the dances, the roster of volunteers, Joyce's advocacy work with governmental offices, support groups, the Saturday recreation program, concerts, theatre and sporting events, and the trips.

But all that dedication was paying off. Not only had the business community gotten on board to help, but more and more students were beginning to understand what was really going on in this mission to meld the communities.

As planned in 1989, the Brigishes from two continents met on a third. Alan, Joyce, Cy, Hal, and Jackie, and Alan's brother, Ron, his wife, Lucy, and their daughter, Jessica (all living in the U.S.), joined Alan's parents, Harry and Fanny, who had traveled from South Africa, in Italy. Cy had just graduated and the trip was a short respite between life phases.

Though Cy had graduated, the social group was thriving, and the family had enjoyed their reunion in Italy, 1989 was a tough year personally for the

---

52 *Westport News*, "Locals Competing in Fall Special Olympics," December 1, 1989

Brigishes. Videolog, the online information company Alan had started five years previously, shut down in 1988, and Alan had been interviewing for jobs. Having been out of the corporate workforce since 1979, he wasn't a "hot property" in that milieu. So, he was doing a little consulting, but money was running low, and they had Jackie headed to college in a few years.

Unable to afford an August rental on the Vineyard while Cy was at camp they, too, became campers, but, at Webb's Camping Area, something they'd never done before. They loaded up sleeping bags, a little tent, and their bikes, and spent a fun few weeks there. Two things were uncomfortable—sleeping on the hard ground—and receiving news, on the campground pay phone, that the last of Alan's interviews did not result in employment.

Two months later, completely out of options, Alan took out a second mortgage on their Weston home, borrowed money from Jackie's college tuition fund, and asked Joyce to quit her sculpting business and take a

deep dive into the unknown by joining him in starting their own newsletter publishing company. The idea was to sell information to people in the publishing business about what was going to be happening to publishing with the advent of the online phenomenon.

So Joyce left Images Gallery and helped Alan found Simba Information, Inc., an information source for publishers. Within a year, the business took off, and they never looked back. They ran the company, and Cy eventually worked for them in the office filing, sorting mail, and being responsible for the weekly 800-piece mailing of the company's newsletters.

As Joyce has said so many times, "You become an advocate, not only for your own child, but for the rest of the population." Manifesting that sentiment, Alan and Joyce hired Matt Klemets, another boy with disabilities (who had been turned down elsewhere) to help out at Simba. "Once Cy showed him how to do what was required, he was fine."[53] Eventually, Alan and Joyce hired Cy, Matt, Larry Shortell, and Anna Lisa Eriksen—all Special Olympians.

---

53 O'Neil, Liz. "Weston's Joyce Brigish—a Very Special Person." *Westport News*, Friday, June 3, 1989.

Chapter 33

THE 1990s
WHAT A DIFFERENCE
A YEAR MAKES

By the beginning of the last decade of the twentieth century, the whole family had created very solid pathways for themselves in their respective endeavors. Things had turned around and Alan and Joyce had bought a vacation house on the Vineyard. No more sleeping on the ground for the month of August.

Once a year, Alan and Joyce would drive Cy up to Syracuse University and drop him off to stay with Hal for a weekend to hang out. The guys, of course, were drinking lots of beer, but Cy would not drink it as he is dead set against imbibing alcohol. "But at a party he would have a Coke—so he had something to drink. And he'd kind of pretend to act a little bit drunk. Of course, he wasn't."

Cy would rather that alcohol never passed his lips. Alan recalled that "one evening the family was out to dinner and Cy asked for a Diet Coke and the waiter thought he'd said 'rum and Coke.' He took a sip and spat it out. He didn't like it. But we kidded him that he'd had alcohol and he was now drunk. And he started to perform—like you wouldn't believe. But he's got a real thing about alcohol. He won't touch it."

Hal said, "Cy would come with me to my friend Nick's party at his

parents' house when we were home from college for the summer. Cy would come along to a lot of places. He was just one of the gang."

But, just for June and July, because every summer day was one day closer to going back to Camp Jabberwocky.

As for the advancement of the social group, the members and volunteers of CLASP had made enormous strides in melding the communities of the area. The first "A Special Day for Special People" event was held at Greens Farm Academy, hosted by the academy's community service club and in conjunction with CLASP. A tenth-grade academy student said, "We learned so much from each other." At the end of the day, it was decided to make it an annual event. "Some of us are going to go with the students to cheer them on when they participate in the regional and state Special Olympics this year." Joyce was beyond delighted with the results of this interchange, and described it as "overwhelming."[54]

The event did continue and close friendships were established between hosts and guests over the years as they enjoyed softball and volleyball games, took part in egg tosses and three-legged races and other activities, and shared a barbecue lunch.

Joyce's dedication and her natural gift for organizing had a magnetic quality. When she put her mind to something, she did indeed find others who trusted her deeply to make change and to blaze new trails. She spear-

54 "A Very Special Day at Greens Farm Academy," Weds, May 2, 1990 (newspaper name missing) (from family scrapbook)

headed or accepted invitations to collaborate with CLASP.

Keeping the young people with disabilities involved in activities that promote fitness, health, improved communication skills, social graces, community-building, and plain old fun was Joyce's mission. She understood from the very beginning of Cy's life how easy it was for a person with disabilities to be marginalized. And indeed, "it takes a village" to teach, organize, and learn from a special population. Fairfield County teemed with people who wanted to make a difference in the lives of others. The variety of activities that the CLASP students enjoyed was due to untold numbers of parents, volunteers, donors, organizations, and organizers who give in so many ways—donating time and moral support, use of venues and funding.

By modeling dedication and generosity, they helped the CLASP members understand what it means to be part of an inclusive and caring community. The Special Olympics team trained at the Y. The Weston Young Women's Club raised money to help organizations that "help people help themselves" and donated generously to them.[55] Many volunteers participated in the games. Westport policemen ran alongside the torch-bearers as part of the opening ceremonies for the Special Olympics when they passed through Westport on the way to the games site.[56] The Westport Policemen's Athletic League (PAL) and the Westport Striped Bass Club jointly sponsored a day of fishing with them, with the gear donated by local tackle shops.

CLASP members appreciated their outings enormously and their own joy at having these experiences added tremendously to the joy of those who sponsored and supported them. The socialization of any one of us is what keeps us working cogs in the collective, a viable part of the community, a giver and a receiver. Feeling the joy of knowing that you belong and are accepted and even celebrated as part of the greater family of humankind is no small thing. Indeed, it may be the very cornerstone of mental health.

---

55 *The Forum*, "Breakfast With Santa Will Benefit Three Groups," November 20, 1991.

56 *Westport News*, "Olympics Torch Blazes Through Westport," June 23, 1989.

Cy had been winning all sorts of medals in the Special Olympics and decorated his room by showcasing those accomplishments. His other favorite things by then, aside from his love of Camp Jabberwocky, were Michael Jackson's music and the TV show *Dallas*. A photo of Larry Hagman as J.R. Ewing in the starring role with posters of Michael and a few other rock stars grace his walls.

All the Brigishes were involved in Joyce's mission, and Jackie's efforts as a volunteer had been noticed as well. In 1990, when she was sixteen years old, she received a 1990 Golden Rule Youth Award (sponsored by Volunteer Center of Southwestern Fairfield County and JC Penney) for "six years of working with CLASP in recreation and Special Olympics programs." JC Penney's Elaine Mykolayko said that year's recipients "show in a very dramatic way what the efforts of volunteers can do for the quality of life in their communities."[57]

Cy had received daily training in courtesy, the whole Brigish family

---

57 *The Advocate,* "Shining Examples" October 4, 1990.

modeling acceptance and support of one another. And as he'd had the rich experience of how it feels when someone cheers you on, it only followed that Cy would be an enthusiastic booster for his peers, rooting heartily for his fellow athletes. Later, when it came time to support his mother, he would be well equipped to do so.

Joyce had these young people doing all sorts of community-based activities. In 1990, CLASP students joined members of the Key Club, the Fairfield County Chorale, and the Kiwanis Club at the Westport YMCA to sing Christmas carols.[58]

In that now-recognizable unwavering attitude, Joyce told a reporter, "It's very important for me to have siblings and family members as well as the community members to be a part of these events. In many cases, siblings don't get involved with their handicapped brother or sister; they've got their own activities that they're involved with.

"That's why it's so incredible to have so many seniors from the high

---

58 *Westport News*, Dec. 21, 1990 (photo description).

school working as volunteers this time of year. They've given up many of their activities to be with us. They've even managed to work around graduation day on Sunday."[59]

About those volunteering to help with CLASP events, Joyce said, "Some are new, others are returning, but all are very important to us."[60]

59 Deal, Mike. "Baseball Game Brings Together Special Friends." *Weston Voice*, June 20, 1991.

60 Ibid.

Chapter 34

BIG CHANGES

B ut "the times, they were a-changin'" for the Brigish offspring. Hal was attending Syracuse University, Jackie would be graduating from high school in 1991, and Cy had graduated from high school in 1989, continued his job at Peter's Market in Weston, was still deeply involved with CLASP activities, and was making preparations for the big switch—to move out.

As Joyce said, "Cy would never *dream* of living with us. He wants to be independent."

STAR Residential Services was an organization serving individuals with developmental disabilities and their families within a six-town area in Fairfield County. Joyce found it very difficult to let Cy go off on his own. She had worked all those years for his independence, but when faced with the reality, she balked. It took every ounce of persuasion on Alan's part to get her to agree.

Though Cy was living on his own, he was still very much a part of CLASP. The Bill Bertin Memorial Baseball Game had been played annually for ten years, an event greatly anticipated. In 1991, Mike Deal wrote, "No one was sure what the score was, but all agreed it must be a tie." Sean Flavin (of high school news fame) was then a college student who still returned summers and worked with the Special Olympics team helping them prepare for the games. The *Weston Voice* reported: "'It's always a tie,' admitted Sean Flavin with a grin. 'It's a great experience. It's satisfying . . . because we care so much for each other. It makes all of us feel good.'"[61]

As with any other group, at the Special Olympics awards banquet of 1991—a lovely dinner catered by Mariane Kolf—formal photos were taken of the honorees in their jackets and ties, and their pretty dresses. This was not a night for sporting the large collection of medals they had won in track and field, gymnastics, bowling, equestrian sports, skiing, baseball, and swimming. Trophies were awarded for superlatives in individual sports and the annual transfer of the plaque for the most supportive family of the year that year was bestowed on the Brigishes. Also notable was that although Joyce would continue as coach of the swim team, she transferred the chairmanship of Special Olympics (which she'd been running "for more than ten years") to Pam Flavin.[62]

The First Annual PAL/CLASP Special Olympic Spring Invitational Swim Meet occurred on April 5, 1992, at the Weston swimming pool. The Westport Police Athletic League (PAL), "a leading non-profit organization providing youth athletic programs and community events," had co-sponsored the Special Olympics for a number of years and devoted their services since 1983. They got together with CLASP to create the swim meet, which included eight teams from across the state competing in thirty-four events. The CLASP swimmers won the day, and they won the trophy— which was described as "our version of the Stanley Cup."[63]

---

61 Ibid.

62 Brubeck, Noreen. "Weston Special Olympics Honored by CLASP Group." *Weston Forum*, November 20, 1991.

63 *The Weston Forum*, "Swim Meet for Special Olympians," April 8, 1992.

Chapter 35

1992

CITIZENSHIP

Alan, Joyce, and Jackie were U.S. citizens; due to her age Jackie had automatically become a citizen when her family moved to the U.S. Hal would take on the task of becoming a citizen much later. Cy was not a U.S. citizen either. When the family traveled internationally, he would have to move through a different customs line, and that upset him.

According to a newspaper article written by Sybil Blau, the family had applied for a green card for Cy because Joyce was adamant that he maintain employment. Twice, in Hartford, his green card application had been torn up "as though his condition made him a non-person." This, of course, infuriated Joyce on a number of levels. Noted the story: "She fought until Cy obtained his green card."

Finally Joyce realized that "Cy would have to go through the process [of becoming a citizen]. There would be no shortcut. And so we said, 'Let's see if we can get there.'"

The news reporter continued: "She [Joyce] fought on when the family was told it was unlikely Cy would qualify for citizenship. And she fought on when the Brigishes sought and were refused exemption from citizenship testing for Cy."[64]

The citizenship test requires knowledge of civics, American history, and the Constitution. With the help of a friend who supplied a book "that explains the Constitution in a way a non-English-speaking person would understand," Joyce and Cy went to work. She made 100 flash cards with questions, written

---

64 Blau, Sybil. "Cyril Brigish: It's Great to be an American." *Weston Forum*, Tuesday, October 20, 1992.

in large letters as Cy has very poor vision and is designated legally blind. Joyce said, "The Constitution was brutal for him. But there was no hurry. It could take five years. As it happened it didn't."

Joyce worked with him every day, doing most of the reading aloud because the print was small and the concepts large. They worked in sequence, one section at a time, until Cy got it—then on to the next section, and then they repeated it all. He memorized the questions and the answers over a period of six months of faithful study.

On the day of the citizenship exam, Cy, who loved to dress up, wore a jacket and tie. Joyce said, "I was a wreck." But Cy was excited. Alan and Joyce knew that if he got more than the three allowed errors, he'd be devastated.

In the one-on-one exam, Cy had to take dictation to prove that he could write, and he had to read aloud and answer questions to prove his capacity to retain information. Twenty questions were posed to Cy for his exam. He aced it! Joyce was grinning broadly when she said, "I think everybody was dancing and loving him."

Cy had his own reason for wanting to become a citizen. He wanted to be able to vote. He registered to vote the morning of October 17, the day after he received his naturalization papers at his allegiance ceremony, just a week after his test. The time span between exam and receiving full citizenship is usually two to three months. But Cy's examiner was so impressed with his diligence and his capabilities, his disabilities notwithstanding, that she expedited the date of the ceremony.[65]

Joyce said, "So, there they were in the fourth-floor courtroom of United States District Court in Bridgeport at 915 Lafayette Boulevard." Ms. Blau reported that the courtroom was filled to capacity with would-be citizens and their families. The individuals took their oath of allegiance and recited the pledge as a group. Alan credited Joyce's perseverance and Cy, who "has a mind like a steel trap," as the foundations for Cy's success.[66]

He even had a visit with Governor Lowell Weicker a few months later.

But citizenship makes one eligible for duty—jury duty. And it didn't take long for a notice to arrive assigning the new citizen an opportunity to perform that duty.

Cy wanted to serve on a jury because he loves the television program *People's Court*, and he thought he'd be on the show. Though Joyce sent the powers-that-be a message stating Cy's disability, he was nonetheless called for jury duty over and over again. Finally, Joyce and Alan had to get an

---

65 Ibid.

66 Ibid.

affidavit from Cy's doctor and letters from various sources confirming that he was disabled and that he shouldn't be called for jury duty. The notices still did not stop. So Joyce thought, *Okay, he'll be on jury duty.* So she took him there. "They took one look and they said, 'Okay, he's excused for life.'"

Chapter 36

THE DAY-TO-DAY

Familiar activities filled Cy's life. He was working at the market, training for Special Olympics, anticipating summer so he could return to camp. His life was filled with learning to live on his own with a roommate. Things were cruising along, except for one thing: He continued to gain weight in spite of the training.

The family took notice when Cy was about thirty. Joyce knew about Weight Watchers but didn't know how to get Cy on board with the idea. Susan Grunthal recalled that Joyce offered him a trip to California if he lost a certain amount of weight.

Joyce said, "Yes, I bribed him." Then she enrolled in Weight Watchers herself, and he decided he would, too. Together, Joyce and Cy worked diligently for months to get him used to a new eating regimen, and eventually to reap the benefits. He lost the weight and the two of them went to San Francisco to visit Cousin Bella, of whom Cy was particularly fond. Susan said Joyce "encouraged him." Joyce said, "If you want to achieve things with him, you've got to do it so that he can be a winner. And then he can win the rest of the way."

Cy learned what works for him and what doesn't. He doesn't eat red meat or pork or cake. But, being human, he'll eat pizza now and again. Cy always called Joyce after his weekly weigh-in, and they'd discuss if he gained or lost. Joyce kept a spreadsheet for him, though he can certainly remember any number of weeks in succession how much he's lost or gained—usually within a pound and a half. If he gained a pound, it concerned him and his mom would ask him what he planned to do the following week to help maintain his weight. He'd been practicing determination his whole life. This was no different. He knew he'd watch what he ate, count his points, and swim more laps at the pool. Having learned to govern what and how much he eats, he lost almost fifty pounds and has kept it off for twenty years.

Joyce said, "The people at Weight Watchers love him." One can imagine

that when he returns in September after his month away at camp, the folks there are very happy to see him. Hal talks about Cy being conscientious about his food, but every now and then . . . "What happens in Vegas, stays in Vegas." Joyce championed that, as well. And Jackie certainly advocates Cy making more of his own decisions, as he keeps Joyce's guidance and the Weight Watchers regime about food choices up front and center.

Chapter 37

1999

DANCING AS A "TURNING POINT"

J oyce took the CLASP group on a trip. A lot of the members love to dance and she found nightclubs and places where they could. But some of the group were underage for some venues and that posed a logistics problem. There was no getting around it—the age range of the group, which extended to about thirty-five years of age, had become a challenge. So, with a new idea in mind, she left CLASP in 1999. Alan recalled that a number of fathers had taken a greater interest in CLASP, and would run it.

Joyce, along with parents, volunteers, and the older members of CLASP, created a new organization, Young Adult Group (YAG), featuring a more mature program to meet the needs of the young adults, specifically the 21-to-35-year-olds. Everyone was of legal age and they "could go anywhere, and

nobody was restricted unless their behavior was inappropriate." Always involved in learning life skills, the new group enjoyed a variety of theatre experiences, went bowling, and traveled several times to various Club Meds, where they could go to the bar and have a beer (except Cy, of course).

Some of the members were quite high-functioning, so Joyce told them, "You're all adults. I need you to come up with ideas of things to do as a group." The whole group went to the Brigishes for an evening of games where about three or four games were set up on tables. Ever keeping an eye on healthy choices, Joyce said, "We had to think of decent food. But they had to be involved in the decisions."

They met about twice a month and went to a show occasionally—the cost being the stumbling block to more frequent theatre events. The organization was set up so that each member paid 50 percent of activity costs, and they were responsible for raising the rest of the funds. As every little bit helped, they redeemed cans regularly, sold chocolates, and were responsible for selling fifty door prize tickets each at their awards banquets.

The founding year of YAG was a busy one socially for the group. Along with Games Night, they had cooking classes and a memorable trip to Paradise Island–Club Med. The photos depict a group of people having the time of their lives. Joyce said, "When I took them all to Club Med, [the chaperones] saw the opportunities for the kids."

The big fundraiser was Joyce's idea. As the family had traveled to Martha's Vineyard every summer and vacationed for a month while Cy was at camp, they'd become friends with drummer Rick Bausman, who was a volunteer at Jabberwocky. Rick has held drumming sessions on Vineyard beaches for years, and drummed with the Jabberwocky campers at the beach as well. The vibrational nature of the drum music can be a full-body experience for anyone, but especially delightful for those who may have one or more senses compromised. Camper Tori (Victoria Conrad), who appeared with Joyce and Cy on the *Vineyard View* show on MVTV, hosted by Ann Bassett,[67] summed up the experience: "The drumming is marvelous. It's very relaxing to be able to be on the beach and not think about anything but being yourself."

Rick came to Connecticut that spring, and together YAG and Rick created the first of four annual Drum-a-thons—a fresh idea for fundraising in the area. YAG members sought sponsors at a price per hour of drumming from 9 am to 9 pm. Rick taught Caribbean and West African rhythms and each member had a partner who could spell him or her during breaks, because those YAG drummers loved to dance! Anyone could bring a drum and join in. And listeners and dancers—guided by Tara Hickman—could attend for a small donation. The finale was a combination of dancers and drummers performing together.

Larry Katz, stepfather of a YAG member, said about YAG, "The organization is fantastic. It gives them a complete social life and many are working and living independently."[68]

67 http://marthasvineyardview.com/video/index.php/dvds-available/ Episode #105 August 14, 2009.

68 Varese, Ashley. "Drumathon Raises Money for Special Young Adults." *The Sunday Hour*, April 2, 2000.

They really did have an enviably good time! In December of 2006, YAG journeyed to Club Med in Punta Cana, Dominican Republic. There was so much to do, and the book Joyce created suggests they did it all:[69] They played tennis and Ping-Pong and learned to play Bocce ball. They exercised in the gym and joined the aerobics classes in the pool. They played in the ocean and the pool. While some played soccer others tried out the roller blades. An alum from Staples High School, Andrew was the archery teacher there, so they practiced hitting the bull's-eye. They visited a school and a cocoa plantation. During the day they tried out the trampoline, swam, buried each other in beach sand, swam again, then changed gears, cleaning up for dinner and dancing, one night to the smooth and raucous tunes of an Elvis Presley impersonator. They all agreed the food was fabulous. And most everyone but Cy enjoyed getting up close and personal with the parrots and monkeys.

69 Brigish, Joyce. *Dominican Republic – Young Adult Group for Special People – December 2-9, 2006*. Photographs contributed by Leys Bostrom, Eleanor Koenig, and JB.

Chapter 38

JABBERWOCKY

Cy loves his annual sojourn at Camp Jabberwocky. During the other forty-eight weeks, he called his mom frequently every day—but never when he's at camp.

Camp Jabberwocky is Cy's world away from the world. He's been at camp for forty summers. They know him well. Nonetheless, he can hornswoggle folks into thinking he's allergic to things he just doesn't want to eat. Joyce readily admitted that he's a "total manipulator. He can do things there that he can't do anywhere else. He walks a lot. He never takes the bus if he can avoid it, so if they go down to the ferry to meet anybody, he walks. Now, he's basically lazy. He wouldn't do that at home. If somebody offered to give him a ride, he'd take the ride in a hurry. At camp, he swims every day. At home he swims around fifty laps two to three times a week."

When it's over and he's had a wonderful time, he's ready to go back home, to return to work. Nonetheless, he begins the countdown of days to the following August session the day he leaves.

Joyce as Jabberwocky Board Member

Clark Hanjian wrote that "we need to upgrade the historical record. People with disabilities rarely achieve more than footnote status in the pages of history. They have been left out of the account because they have been left out of the culture. Jabberwocky, though, is a different culture. It is a place where disabled folks are at the center of a community rather than at the periphery. Jabberwocky is not the same old story."[70]

At Jabberwocky, Joyce had found like-minded people whose heartfelt actions mirrored their beliefs and a whole heap of others had supplied the armature on which the camp runs.

The story of Camp Jabberwocky, Mr. Hanjian continued, "is a record of experiments and risks. A portrait of cooperation. Jabberwocky is a tale of bountiful harvest from a few scattered seeds. It is an epic of generosity and thanksgiving. Stories like this are crucial to the existence of humanity. They remind us of what great things are possible in our limited days."

For about thirty years, Joyce's capacity at Camp Jabberwocky was as a parent; for about the last eight years she was also a board member. She founded and organized the annual 5K race to raise awareness as well as funds. One of Joyce's tasks was writing thank-you notes to let donors on every level know how deeply their gifts were appreciated in keeping the camp running.

Joyce was always trying to increase awareness of the wonderful place that is camp, to increase the integration of the Jabberwocky community with the wider Island population—which, because camp runs only in summer, can top 100,000 on any given day.

After several years on the board, she initiated camp invitations to two groups of eight or ten women (not necessarily people she knew) to join her, one group for a day in July and the other in August. "They'd help me make lunch for the campers—sandwiches or salads—easy lunch, and it's a good way to expose people to this population."

Joyce gave tours for any of the women who'd not been to camp,

---

70 Hanjian, Clark. *Camp Jabberwocky – A Brief History of the Martha's Vineyard Cerebral Palsy Camp.* Martha's Vineyard Cerebral Palsy Camp, Vineyard Haven, MA. 1989. P. 2.

showing them where the campers and counselors, doctors, and director live, and she'd tell them about the variety of activities at camp. "It just gives them an experience of what the camp is really like," Joyce said. Moreover, it substantiates for any visitor what Clark Hanjian highlights as "not the same old story."

Chapter 39

TWENTY-FIRST CENTURY

T he new millennium brought all sorts of change to coincide with established routines. Though 1989 had been a struggle, it also had been a watershed year for the family. When Alan and Joyce sold

Simba in 1996, they were employing sixty-five full-time staff. Twenty-two years later, the company is still active.

Camp Jabberwocky and Special Olympics were still summer highlights. Alan and Joyce, who vacationed every August while Cy was at camp, sold their summer home in one island town and Joyce designed a home that they built in a neighboring town, with the intent of moving there permanently someday. The golden retriever, Rugby, was a handsome dog, and he and Cy entered the Dog Show at the Martha's Vineyard Agricultural Fair.

The siblings had ample opportunity to spend benchmark time together. In 2001, when Jackie married Dan Parker (who had been Cy's one-to-one in Special Olympics), her brothers and Dan's brothers, Ray and Matt, were groomsmen.

The following year Cy, Hal, and Jackie made the eighteen-hour flight to

Cape Town to have one last visit with their grandfather, Harry, who was in ill health.

That first decade brought so many changes and challenges. But Special Olympics and Camp were still annual highlights.

2009 was a banner year for the family. Alan's book *Breathing in the Buddha* had come out. He was asked to appear on MVTV's *Vineyard View* show, hosted by Ann Bassett. Cy and Tori (Victoria Camden) and

Joyce were also interviewed for a separate episode representing Camp Jabberwocky.

Though cerebral palsy confines her to a wheelchair and she has slightly labored speech, Tori is articulate and was college-bound after camp. "I'm determined to be as independent as possible and there's nothing wrong with asking for help. One thing I've learned from my disability is that you have to have patience with people when you're trying to explain to them how to do something. Because with me, I'm amazingly only impaired physically, so I can picture myself getting ready for bed. But it's sometimes difficult to describe to people how to do it. So I have to be patient and learn how to talk them through it. And that's one of the most rewarding parts of my life, because I can teach someone how to do something." Regarding the counselors, she said, "They do it out of the kindness of their hearts, which I think demonstrates true character and true compassion for others."[71]

Cy's Travels

For years, Hal's annual birthday present for Cy has been to bring him to Virginia from Connecticut on the train. Joyce put him on the train and Cy had a cell phone. He'd travel nine hours on his own. Then Hal picked him up at his destination and they'd go out to dinner and take in a UVA game and visit friends. These days, Hal picks Cy up in Connecticut and they go to New York

---

71 http://marthasvineyardview.com/video/index.php/dvds-available/ Episode #105 August 14, 2009.

City. Last year, they went with friends to a Yankees game in New York, and sang to the oldies in the car. This year they included Cy's camp counselor, Sam, and a fine time was had by all. When the festivities wind down, Hal drives Cy back to his condo, and the next day, heads home.

Employment

Family friends hold a deep respect for Alan and Joyce because they had made it very clear to Cy what they expected of him, which helped him under-stand his potential. Judy Machanik stressed that not only did they teach him responsibility, "but the poten-tial for learning something that he didn't know before, how to interact with the public that didn't know him, and who he didn't know. I think that whole sense of giving him the tools to be a responsible member of society, if you will, was so criti-cal to his development. He loved to work. He was proud of the work that he did. I remember my kids used to talk to him about the jobs that he was doing."

Alan and Joyce were adamant about employment. Hal said, "Gotta work, kid!" was their message. So Hal got a job at fourteen at the George-town Saloon washing dishes and working his way up. Cy occasionally would come in and help out with the dishwashing.

In the summer, visiting before or after his camp session or when he was on the Island with his par-ents, Cy would work at Chilmark Chocolates for a spate.

In high school, Cy had a job at a travel company, and his boss offered him a job after he graduated. Cy worked for a watchmaker, attaching

the wristbands to the watches. But his eyesight was too poor for the work. He worked at Peter's Market in Weston for a long time, and enjoyed all the people coming in and out, so many of whom he knew. He always relayed messages of greeting to his parents, naming everyone who'd shopped that day who had asked for them.

In a *Weston Voice* article, Steve Foreman, his employer at Peter's Market in Weston, says he is a hard worker, "pleasant and capable."

"During the past four years he has worked at the market, Cy can be seen sweeping, restocking, bagging groceries and carrying packages to cars for shoppers. He also has a special gift for remembering names."

The news reporter continued: "When Cy first began to work at the market, Steve Foreman received a number of phone calls. 'They were all positive.'"[72]

In addition to working at the local market three afternoons a week, Cy helped out at Joan and Joyce's gallery assisting with mailings for five years, from 1984 to1989. He also worked at a supermarket, Zeytinia, and for a long time bagging groceries at another supermarket that eventually closed down.

Joyce would always make sure that he had more than one part-time job, so, as in the case of the market closing, he would remain employed somewhere and not stay at home watching television.

At Petco, he stocked shelves and kept them tidy and clean, swept the store and emptied the rubbish. He used to clean the fish tanks, though he was not fond of that. There are birds there as well, which Cy does not like at all. That

72 Hurley, Johanna. "Local Man Overcomes Many Obstacles." *Weston Voice*, Feb. 13, 1992.

may have something to do with Basil having had free range over the house when Cy was small.

At work, Cy keeps little to himself, so, at home, he also reports "good news" when he receives a tip or finds a coin on the floor, also categorized as "a tip." Gregarious Cy regularly bumps into people he knows, family friends, and sometimes Jackie's friends from school, and relates his conversations, all meetings, and content of messages, as in "They sent their love." What Cy offers in conversation is accurate updates on his family. Joyce said, "He knows what he's talking about. He's pretty serious."

One's place in the world is affirmed by connections, and Cy is a master at making and maintaining connections.

Cy's Associative Mind

Joyce recalled, "When he worked for us in the publishing company, he was close to all the employees of the company. He had names for each of them from the television show, *90210*," referring to each of them only by the characters' names, except for Chris Elwell, who Cy called—"

Here Cy chimed in: "*My Senior Partner.*"

Alan and I (the author) went to a signing the summer of 2010 for a book we did together, *Martha's Vineyard—Now & Zen*. Alan's appearance was showcased out front, but I didn't get a mention. Our hostess claimed surprise at my presence.

A few days later, when Cy was visiting his parents after camp, his dad and I were on the phone, and Alan jokingly asked me what it feels like to be "chopped liver." After we'd hung up Cy asked his dad why he would call somebody "chopped liver." Alan explained. The next time I walked in the door, Cy greeted me with his signature smooch on the cheek and, grinning, said, "Hello Chopped Liver." And he's been calling me Chopped Liver ever since.

A sense of humor develops only through social engagement. Humor requires intelligence and a circle of communication and it's in the sharing that we discover what is and is not funny. Cy has a great sense of timing and comic understanding—a deeper natural sense of humor than one might suspect at first meeting. Cy is a funny man who descends from a fun-loving family.

Alan and Cy went to see the movie *In and Out*, starring Kevin Kline. It's set in the 1970s and is about a teacher who hasn't realized that he's gay, though others have guessed. At an event, he's outed to the whole school. In support, a student stands up and says, "I'm gay." And another student stands up and says, "I'm gay." And so on. Cy stood up in the middle of the movie and said, "I'm gay." Alan said, "The whole film audience just erupted."

Cy's Grace and Humor

For many years, friend Olive Tomlinson had a New Year's Day luncheon buffet. Her small house was crammed, and the buffet was a groaning board of delights. "The regulars" all knew where they'd be on January 1, and Cy wouldn't miss it, but Olive always invited new people.

Cy was usually there with Alan and Joyce and was part of the party. We'd have a conversation and maybe talk about Christmas. I sensed when people gave us sidelong glances, perhaps not being used to socializing with an adult with Down syndrome.

Olive always collected information from her party guests about their experiences during the previous year. She categorized those experiences: travel, achievements, new creative works, and replaced body parts, to name a few.

When Olive, who is a born comedienne, took to her "platform" on a chair, she tossed out accolades to all, in delightfully humorous fashion, and always included Cy's latest achievement—his swimming prowess or medals earned at Special Olympics.

And when "Mr. Saturday Night" immediately stood up, the uninitiated registered a look of mild terror as perhaps they wondered what was coming. Then, simultaneously gracious and off-handed, Cy would say, "Olive, you are a piece of work!" charming the crowd in a single statement.

Cy enjoys the routine of Weight Watchers. Every week he and his mom would talk about what he'd like to eat for the week, each meal and dessert. She'd punch it into the computer and fax it to him. And he'd substitute equivalents if he didn't

have a particular food item in the house. It remained very important to Joyce that Cy continue to take responsibility for calculating his weight, so they kept records of that as well, though Cy can remember the numbers for consecutive weeks.

Cy's home today is run on that same principle he learned as a child, sharing responsibilities, cleaning, preparing food, and cleaning up, with his roommate and caregiver. Mostly, they cook and eat at home. But occasionally, he enjoys an evening out. And going bowling is a favorite pastime.

Hal said, "We're very fortunate that Cy is as independent as he is. And a lot has to do with just the genetics that he has and a lot has to do with what he's been taught."

Joyce is no longer here to guide him, but Cy continues to attend his weekly weigh-ins, then calls his dad with the number, and conscientiously maintains his weight. Because Cy still has medical issues requiring attention, Alan maintains a different spreadsheet that includes health, pain management, and diet. Ongoing chronic stomach issues which require frequent medical checkups sideline Cy every now and then. So he exercises daily

and has regular physical therapy. Ro (Rosann) Salvo, Cy's #2 helper—is compassionate and competent and helps Cy with his food choices, reporting to Alan on the spreadsheet. Through all the time spent in doctor's offices, emergency rooms, and hospital stays, Cy keeps on keeping on. With all the support he's received these five decades, Cy has the experience of knowing he has worth in this world and he appreciates others. He admires some of his doctors a great deal, and lets them know it. Joyce said, "He gave his podiatrist (who he loves) a gold medal that he'd won at Special Olympics, and this man just burst into tears. And he did the same thing with his surgeon who operated on his last hernia."

Cy's Socialization

"What you get by achieving your goals is not as important as who you become by achieving your goals." So said Henry David Thoreau. Joyce, natural teacher that she was, worked on goal-setting with Cy from the earliest days of his life. Sometimes tiny goals, as with any child, like learning all the small sequences of dressing oneself, were the order of the day. What she knew

was that he had to feel the thrill of success, and so she made the goals manageable and achievable, for skill-building as well as for developing behaviors that would show him to be more like others than different.

Joyce's commitment to Cy's socialization resulted in his ability to be thoughtful and very observant. Joyce pointed out poor behavior and good behavior and taught him what he should not do—"such as so-and-so is doing"—and how to behave instead, as well. And he practiced, and thus learned to think critically. Any bona fide teacher will tell you that active learning has staying power. As well as the intellect, and the senses, the body registers information through practice. Because Cy was so familiar with social engagement and Joyce made certain the community was as involved with Cy as he was involved in the community, he enjoys conversation, is gregarious and welcoming. Cy has impeccable manners, is gracious and humorous, and handles himself well in social situations. He has been taught to have a work ethic and is hardworking, though, as Joyce confirmed, he is not innately a self-starter. He once may have been unwittingly designated as

"uneducable," but he was given a chance by those who loved him well, and the proof of that continuous opportunity to attempt and achieve is manifest in the qualities of the man he has become.

Joyce said, "I always said, 'I'm paving the way for the next generation' and now we're a few generations even away from that, I'm not envious of it. I think it's wonderful that the kids today have so many more opportunities than they had in Cy's time."

Paving the way is most certainly what she did. About Cy's social training, Joyce said, "It *was* time-consuming. But it was important. It was so important that he did the right things, that he acted appropriately, that he, at this age, can go anywhere and nobody would stare at him as they did when he was younger. And nobody would point fingers at him."

Joyce continued, "In both his jobs, especially the job in the restaurant, people have said to me, 'He is so polite. He is so amazing.' They go to this restaurant because they love to see him there and talk to him. And so that makes me feel, well, it was all worthwhile."

Brother Hal says Cy's mellowed with age and is quieter than he used to be. On a ride to the Vineyard with Hal, his girlfriend, Katie, and her daughter, Sera, Cy was very low-key. They found the Pandora station that played music from the late 1970s and '80s when they were boys, and "that was all she wrote" for being quiet in the back seat. The whole carful burst into song. Cy knew all the words and played the drum riffs, dancing in his seat. Hal said, "Kind of brings you back to being a kid, him with his record player—especially seeing him playing those drums. He knew exactly where the drum part was."

Sister Jackie says, "Cy's just a good person. And that's because of the way he was brought up. The loving, guiding support he's always been given was just so important. All the acceptance within the community, the family and the extended family—beyond when he was a baby when they first found out he had Downs—everybody always loved Cy."

Jackie taught alongside Joanne Cassano, the same special education teacher that Cy had had for many years who became an inclusion teacher in her classroom. His PE teacher was still there. The principal who hired her had been the assistant principal for Cy. So many people there knew Cy, and always asked about him, and loved it when he came to something at the school. He was just *remembered*.

Cy is gentle, and all report that he's fabulous with babies. Nonetheless, Alan said, "He's as strong as an ox—he's also double-jointed. When he and either his brother-in-law or his brother have a wrestling match on our couch, look out! He uses feet, legs, and he's stronger than they are. Even though he's very kind of floppy-jointed, he's powerful and has a natural strength."

The support and playfulness of the siblings carries on, even though they are quite grown. And with niece and nephews, the dynamics are still the same. With the extension of the family through Jackie's and Dan's three children, the playfulness of the whole clan has been magnified.

Chapter 40

2016

DIAGNOSIS

In 2003, Joyce was diagnosed with breast cancer. After surgery and radiation, she had a good recovery and was doing well for a number of years.

However, she developed a stiffening of her neck, resulting in agonizing pain. Her head and neck movement diminished and continued to worsen during the next dozen years. As is Alan's wont, he researched every possible cause, and together they pursued every avenue and visited a variety of specialists to get her some relief. A lesser woman would have taken to her bed, but a somewhat compromised Joyce is still a stoic force to reckon with. Within the next four years, Joyce had one and then the other knee replaced.

An old adage suggests that if you're feeling under the weather or down in the dumps, do something kind for someone else, and it will lift you both up. Joyce most certainly embodied that saying, volunteering in a number of capacities and keeping commitment on boards, administering the Camp Jabberwocky annual 5K run, and taking the family golden retriever Zach to the elder housing facility, Windemere, as a therapy dog. She and Zach enjoyed it immensely and would return beaming from the warm welcome they always received from the residents there. Family gatherings and birthdays remained all-important, and in spite of her discomfort, it was always "family first."

Joyce developed breathing problems in the winter of 2016, and that February, Joyce received the devastating news of a diagnosis of terminal mesothelioma. She said she'd tried to talk to Cy for years about the fact that his parents would be leaving him one day, but that Hal and Jackie would be here. He didn't seem to be able to accept it.

Cy has lost several friends to cancer, and he's had it himself. So he knows that

some people die from it, but that he survived it. The whole family and anyone who knows the Brigishes were concerned for how this would affect the two of them.

Joyce started her chemotherapy sessions the following May. Band-Aids upset Cy. So, to minimize his distress over his mother's condition, Joyce never let him see one on her skin covering the site of an injection. He did not accompany her to infusions, never saw the port. And because Cy retains details, the family tried not to talk too much about things that might upset him, like Joyce's condition. Nonetheless, he had nightmares that his mother had died. "I don't want to lose you," he'd said in tears on the phone.

That month we started the interviews for this book. Joyce was in constant pain, but indomitable as ever. She would sit and talk with me for an hour or so—as long as she could—sipping Perrier trying to keep off the chemo-induced nausea, until she simply just had to sleep.

Joyce was receiving a phone call from Hal, Jackie, and Cy daily, which was typical for Cy anyway. Joyce said, "Cy's pretty sad about me. He asks me every day how I'm feeling. And I always say 'I'm fine.' And then he says, 'Oh, great. But, you know, you're not really fine. You are not getting better as fast as I got better from my cancer.' 'That's okay. I'm getting better, Cy.' He says, 'Good, good, good.' It obviously worries him. On his own, he'll write a card to me, 'Get better soon. I love you. Cy.'"

Lending support is a sign of Cy's genuine innate kindness, and a reflection of his experience. People have "showed up" for Cy for decades, and he knows what a lovely feeling it is to have friends and family make the effort to be there for each other.

On a still night at the end of August in 2016, I joined Cy and his parents at a small diner at an airfield for dinner. Cy had just given me a greeting of a hug and a kiss and said, "Come inside. I'll show you where we can sit." Just then, the final member of our party, Cy's favorite counselor, Sam, from Camp Jabberwocky, drove up. Cy and Sam hadn't seen each other since camp had let out eight days before. She'd since completed a round trip to the Midwest to see her dad, who had required some assistance. Having just arrived on the Island, she'd headed straight for the diner.

When the two clapped eyes on each other, there was much bubbly laughter and hugging, not the typical counselor-camper relationship. This was a genuine adult kinship of like spirits. Cy took the time to introduce me to Sam, and then we took our seats. Their conversation was lively and Cy was atypically animated, as he is only when with his nearest and dearest, or on stage where the audience as a unit is a loved one. They reminisced about summer, talked of their activities—traditions upheld and new adventures—and made plans for the following year.

I watched Joyce watching them, a look of deep satisfaction on her face, smiling though stoically experiencing some relentless pain from her mesothelioma.

Alan asked Sam why a young woman takes the summer off to volunteer as a counselor, living in a cabin with adult campers, and taking responsibility for the welfare of a number of them daily. She said, "Because I've never had so much fun in all my life as I do at camp. So many funny things happen, and though I'm there as a caregiver, I'm aware that we are all teachers and learners both."

She continued, "One day at camp I received a package from my dad, who'd suffered a stroke. I made the mistake of opening it up while we were all having a meal. When I saw all the crayon drawings he'd made for me, in his post-stroke reality, I burst into tears and couldn't stop crying. There I was in the midst of a group of people for whom I am responsible—I'm there to take care of them!—and yet, I was surrounded by people consoling me. A more loving and compassionate group cannot be found anywhere. *They* were consoling *me*."

Cy laid his hand on her arm and, so quietly and tenderly, said, "Aw, Sam."

And there's the end result of what happens when the mother of a child in whom she has seen the spark of intelligence, and his sense of humor, and innate kindness, is told not to waste her time on him, that he is not educable, that he's *only* Down syndrome—and she says, "I think not," and sets to work.

So began the journey of Joyce's adult life, giving birth to a child with Down syndrome, yet, against all odds and in the face of much opposition, welcoming everyone to the table, exploring parameters, teaching people their valued place in the human family, holding the bar as high as possible for learners, athletes, artists, standing by to see them rejoice in discovering their own capabilities, guiding, teaching, modeling, advocating, cheering, and applauding, and saying "You can!"—determined, unwavering, formidable, and loving.

With the steadfast help of Alan, Hal, and Jackie, dear friends, and so many others during the last fifty years, her boy-child has been given every opportunity to understand he had the right to set goals, to reach and grow and become. And quite often, arms flung wide, now *Cy* is the gentleman saying, "Welcome to the table."

Joyce deeply appreciated all the kindnesses she received from a multitude of sources. Though she had surgery in July, it did not improve the quality of her life. Well-wishes poured in from friends and family around the globe. Adriana Stadecker, a longtime friend of Joyce's. shared the following about their relationship and conversations during that time.

"Many times we spoke on the phone or went out for lunch and talked about our grandchildren or our next trips. At other times however, we had more metaphysical conversations about life.

"As we are hit by difficult situations (son w/Down syndrome, cancer etc. . . .) one can ask oneself why are these things happening to me and it is difficult not to feel like a victim. Being a victim was never our choice. Instead, we felt that there must be learning opportunities in these hard experiences, and that by focusing on them, we somehow got more in touch with a renewed sense of purpose.

"Nothing lasts forever. Joyce and I would check in on any given day and one of us would have had a bad night, or have a bad headache, etc. . . . We knew, though, that if not tomorrow, probably the day after, our misery would be relieved and we would continue with our planned activities. That was always a comforting feeling. However, there came a point in Joyce's fight with her mesothelioma that the good days became less frequent and it was quite difficult to find comfort in herself. That was the time when family and friends played an even bigger role in her life. A phone call from Jackie, a visit from Hal and Cy gave more meaning to each day."

Wanting Cy to be able to be with Joyce in the final weeks of her life, and to experience the dying process as a part of life, Alan brought Cy to her bedside and let him just sit with her. Cy would talk to her when she could no longer communicate.

Joyce died on October 9, 2016. Her celebration of life and burial were the following Thursday. Friends and family flew in from all across the United States and England. Each of the family delivered a portion of her eulogy and Cy was the final speaker.

"I'm sad. I'm very, very sad." And then after a long pause, Cy stepped down from the microphone. Gently patting the coffin, he said, "I love you, Mom. But, now it's time to say 'goodbye.'"

If ever there was a parent-child connection that spanned eternity . . .

Chapter 41

JOYCE AND CY

Joyce was indeed remarkable. Her mission—to teach as many people as possible about the joys and benefits of inclusion for everyone, to help people with disabilities reach beyond expectations, and to blend communities of people, which she manifested in word and deed—has left an indelible mark on many of us. Her absence is palpable, and in concert with Alan, Hal, Jackie, and Cy, countless volunteers, risk-takers, and people with disabilities willing to embrace change—her legacy is that she really did make the world a better place.

Joyce was formidable when acting on behalf of others. Her communication was clear, sometimes abrupt. She reassured, but she did not coddle. Her work on behalf of people, with and without disabilities, was not a job, or an avocation, but a mission, and she fully understood she could not inspire growth and change without the help of hundreds, most likely thousands willing to give their time in the name of change—individuals as well as organizations ready to get on board.

Her natural instincts for (and actions to provide) what we all need—attention, role models, practice setting goals and support in helping us reach them, opportunity, cheering on, inclusion, family, community, and love, healthy food, and regular exercise—were unswerving. She demanded that people be met at their learning edge to develop physically, intellectually, socially to the best of their ability and she did not ask of anyone what she would not do herself.

Her steadfast dedication to engaging the lives of so many people on both sides of the proactive equation resulted in an enrichment of everyone involved.

Joyce was a humanitarian with the gift of meeting challenges head-on and the ability to dig deep to find the grit to meet the next one. As Erik Weihenmayer said: "It's about that light inside and using that as fuel and vision to power you through a lot of challenges." Joyce had that light that would not be dimmed. The motto for Cy must have been her mantra as well. When faced regularly with what initially might have seemed insurmountable, she was more than courageous to embody the attitude of "Yes, I can."

One of the ways that Joyce embodied her activism was in the respectful personal interchange with each child and adult with disabilities she encountered. Though she was somewhat contained and more than a little shy herself, her warmth and her support helped people understand what she was about—offering the opportunity to explore and reach one's potential—her own guidance and firmness in expressing and upholding expectations of appropriate behavior were part and parcel to that end—the amalgamation of communities to do more than tolerate, but rather to engage, enjoy, and learn from one another.

Cy still spends four weeks in August at Camp Jabberwocky, as he has for the past forty years. Living in an apartment with a caregiver and a roommate, Cy has the luxury of the best care. He holds down three part-time jobs for eleven months of the year. He also travels on public transportation with someone dropping him off at his departure point. He might be able to negotiate more but for his poor vision.

Cy carries on with his schedule. A genetic propensity for aging joint issues means a bothersome hip. His jobs keep him on his feet, so he's given up his job at Petco (where he worked for more than fifteen years) for a desk job filing. He's still swimming a couple of days a week and he, roommate Matt, and Cathy (who Cy says is like his second mother) keep a steady schedule of making food choices, shopping, and cooking healthy foods to maintain his weight. Life goes on.

But, grieving is rarely a tidy process. Cy misses his mom, as do all of Joyce's friends and family and colleagues. She was a force—no question. Though his day-to-day routine is adhered to, he's lost his greatest champion, and that means a vast change in not having the comfort of hearing Joyce's voice.

Cy has grown quieter in the last few years. The old Cy, of course, is still there, though not always so evident. What has not changed is that Cy is looking forward to camp just as he has for forty years. There, in that place like no other, life is lived through a kaleidoscopic lens, sparks of joy careening about.

If you can't make this year's Camp Jabberwocky extravaganza, catch another. In this weighty world, it's a sweet opportunity to wander down Joyce's Way to see Cy and his friends cooking up some high hilarity spiced with wonder and gladness – a veritable feast for the heart.

Afterword

Did you know that she dropped a car battery on another child's foot, and beat all the boys at marbles? Her exasperated mother sent her to a convent boarding school. Hidden behind that sweet exterior, there was a mighty will to do things Joyce's way.

Let me tell you about Joycie Hirshovitz, whom I met in 1963 when we were students—she, studying to become a mathematics teacher and I, an electronics engineer. We lived in the same apartment block in Johannesburg, South Africa, and we met one day in the lobby. We became friends, and when I discovered that her bedroom was directly below mine, I conspired with her father to let me build a little intercom system that I snuck under her bed with wires trailing out of the window and up the outside of the building to my bedroom.

Later that day, I switched it on to hear her giving her father lip over some transgression. "Joyce," I said, "that is no way to talk to your father." She let out a scream and dove under the bed to see if I was hiding there, only to find a little black box with wires. After she got over the shock, we agreed to leave it in place so that we could have late-night chats about our respective dates on a Saturday night. In no time, we began dating. I owe a lot to that little box with wires.

From the beginning, we always jointly problem-solved over money and always supported each other. We easily agreed on what we liked and did not like. If we both liked something we did it as a team, but, if one did not want to do it, we did not do it. We respected each other for who we each were. We tried hard to be patient and accept each other's shortcomings. We shared a deep intimacy. We were grateful for each other. These actions, in no small measure, were due to our acceptance of each other, "just as we were." In my view, this is the secret of our great marriage.

Joyce ALWAYS put the needs and wants of others ahead of her own, except that if she wanted frozen yogurt, it took priority. She embodied the ethos of kindness and generosity. She spent a great amount of time and energy making my life easier. I am grateful beyond words to have had Joycie Hirshovitz as my best friend and lover.

And then there was Cy. It is hard to describe their relationship as anything but one of the deepest, sweetest, and abiding love. Of course, Hal, Jackie, and I all shared in this experience and it bonded our family, like a rock. But Joyce and Cy—they were something special.

And on a final, deeply personal note, many people asked Joyce to write down what she had done and what she had learned. Writing in the first person was not something she would ever do, but in the last few months of her life she asked our dear friend, Susan Klein, if she would take on the task of interviewing and writing it all down. And, after fifty years of observing the love between Cy and Joyce, I thought it would be a fitting tribute to include some of the thousands of photographs that I took of them. So, in a sense it's our final project together—Joyce's story illustrated by my observations.

Alan Brigish
West Tisbury
May 2018

Bibliography

Bowman-Krum, Mary, Ed.D. *Everything You Need to Know About Down Syndrome*. NewYork: Rosen Publishing Group, 2000.

Brigish, Cy, and Conrad, Victoria, interview by Ann Bassett/*Vineyard View*, MVTV, August 14, 2009 - Camp Jabberwocky; http://www.mvtv.org/video-on-demand-castus/

Hanjian, Clark. *Jabberwocky: A Brief History of the Martha's Vineyard Cerebral Palsy Camp*. Vineyard Haven, MA, 1989.

Parent, Michael. "The Pinch-Hitter." In *Heroes and Villains in American Literature*, edited by Henry I. Christ, 470. New York: Amsco School Publications, 1996.

Powell, Jillian. *Luke Has Down's Syndrome*. London: Evans Brothers Limited, 2005.

Soper, Kathryn Lynard Soper, ed. *Gifts: Mothers Reflect on How Children with Down Syndrome Enrich Their Lives*. Bethesda, MD: Woolbine House, 2007.

Stuve-Bodeen, Stephanie. *We'll Paint the Octopus Red*. Bethesda, MD: Woolbine House, 1998.